williams Books
16369
12/97
24.95

The Crown Devon
Collectors Handbook

Ray Barker FAIE IABC

Francis Joseph
ISBN 1-870703-22-7

Acknowledgements

My thanks to all the Crown Devon collectors who loaned pieces from their collections for photographic purposes. My thanks to the Crown Devon people from Cumbria in the North to Chelwood Gate inthe South, from Cardiff in Welsh Wales to Scunthorpe on Humberside and to our friends in the Midlands who have helped to collect and compile hundreds of prices from which the price guides have been compiled.

Cover picture
This illustrates the vast range of products by the Fielding factory. Back row: The Victorian Girl 'Sunday Best' worth around £300, the ever popular Rio Rita (£600-£700), and one of the rare pair of ewers in Wild Roses pattern (£300-£350). In the centre, one of a pair of Peacock vases by Stuart (£300-£350), a Matta Sung pot pourri jar (£200). In front: a preserve jar (£30), vellum salt cellar (£15), small dog (£30), and Sutherland figure Gina (£100-£120).

© 1997 Francis Joseph Publications

Published in the UK by
Francis Joseph Publications
15 St Swithuns Road, London SE13 6RW
Telephone: 0181 318 9580

Typeset by E J Folkard Computer Services
199 Station Road, Crayford, Kent DA1 3QF

Printed in Great Britain by
Greenwich Press, London SE7 England

ISBN 1-870703-22-7

To Irene, the girl in ATS uniform,
who waved goodbye as my troopship
sailed down the Clyde
just a few hours after our
wedding in 1943.

About the author

1943 – Ray and Irene Barker at their wedding at Colne in Lancashire.

1996 – Ray and Irene in their garden at Beckmere near the Malvern Hills.

Ray Barker, a journalist for more than half a century, retired in June 1990 and his colleagues at Volkswagen UK gave him a new typewriter so that he could work on a little longer to produce a book about Crown Devon, his hobby for a decade.

Born in Mirfield, Yorkshire, in 1920, Ray joined the *Dewsbury District News* in 1936 as a junior reporter. He served in the RAF during the war then continued his career with the *Yorkshire Evening News*, then the *Daily* and *Sunday Express*. He became chief sub-editor of the *Manchester Evening Chronicle* and then the *Lancashire Evening Post* before going into industrial journalism with Leyland Motors in 1969.

He was managing editor of the *British Leyland Mirror* from 1973 to 1977 when it was voted 'The best company newspaper in Britain'. Ray retired for the first time in 1984 but went back to launch *Volkswagen Link* and make it Britain's best company newspaper by 1990. Ray became the first industrial editor to win the BAIE top title with two different papers.

Contents

Introduction

My first book *The Crown Devon Story* was published in November 1991 and sold out within two years. Requests for the book continued to pour in not only from collectors in this country but from South Africa, New Zealand, Australia and North America and one even came from East Berlin!

With a second book in mind, I continued to collect information on Crown Devon helped by scores of collectors – and dealers, too. And Crown Devon, or CD as most of us know it – is full of surprises. I have been collecting Fieldings and Crown Devon for 15 years and I am still finding pieces that I didn't know existed owing to the lack of company records for the first 50 years.

My second book *The Crown Devon Collectors Handbook* tells the story of Simon Fielding and Company in a nutshell but majors on the vast range of products which came from the Devon Pottery. The Crown Devon name was synonymous with quality for around 100 years and the products of the factory in Sutherland Street, Stoke-on-Trent, are sought after more than they have ever been.

And as more and more people have joined the hunt for Crown Devon over the years, so the price has continued to rise.

What IS the right price? There will always be bargains. They make collecting so enjoyable and there will always be people prepared to pay that little bit extra for a piece they really want. This book has tried to strike a happy medium. Good luck – and good hunting.

Ray Barker

NB: This was the advice given to me by a veteran collector: "If you see something you like, examine it for damage or restoration. If its right then haggle a bit . . . and a bit more . . . and if then you can afford the price . . . buy it. You won't go far wrong." That is as good advice today as it was 15 years ago.

Abbreviations used in this book

RN   Registered number
PN   Pattern Name or number
PG   Price Guide
BS   Backstamp
R   Rare
VR   Very rare

A Century of Ceramics

Simon Fielding

The Crown Devon story started in the latter half of the last century when Simon Fielding, an expert in dogs and poultry, and who worked at Trentham Hall, the seat of the Duke of Sutherland, put his life savings into the Railway Works in Sutherland Street, Stoke-on-Trent. But by 1878 the bailiffs came in and it was Simon's son, Abraham, who stepped in to save the company.

Majolica ware was in fashion and Abraham started to produce it in abundance. The firm flourished and in 1892 a whole row of cottages came down to make way for new ovens, a warehouse, and printing and painting shops.

Towards the end of the century, Abraham introduced a superb Vellum ware which was an immediate success. It was at about this time that Fieldings introduced the name "Crown Devon" which appeared on a variety of patterns although it was not until 1911 that Railway Works became Devon Pottery.

Scores of new patterns were introduced on a vast range of products and one which became very popular with customers was Royal Devon with its white and red flowers tinged with blue. Month by month, Fieldings brought in more and more royal patterns, including Royal Essex, Royal Sussex, Royal York, Royal Scotia and Royal Suffolk to name but a few. Surprisingly, there was no Royal Staffordshire.

After the first world war, fashions changed again. In came many of the Crown Devon fancy tableware designs. It was the decade of art deco, an era of fancies and novelties with musical jugs and mugs and even a musical chamber potty and throughout the Thirties the range proved to be one of the best money-spinners the firm had ever had.

The decade also saw the introduction of lustreware in ruby, green and blue, of the Ivrine series of figures, dogs and birds and even an elephant. There were the popular Sutherland figures and at the top of the range, the figurines modelled by Kathleen Parsons, a young and talented artist from Sheffield.

Her art deco figures included nudes in various poses were exported to South Africa, Australia, New Zealand and Canada.

Ironically, it was in Sydney in 1942 that Kathleen last saw a collection of her models

Abraham Fielding

Above: Part of the Crown Devon exhibition at ceramics specialists Cleghorn and Harris of Cape Town, South Africa, in 1939. In the foreground are several figures by Kathleen Parsons. A collection like that today would probably fetch in the region of £5000/$9000!

Below: A rare 1930s picture of Kathleen Parsons who designed and modelled Art Deco figures at her studio in Sheffield. She sold them to Reg Fielding for a few pounds each. Today figures such as those in the picture are worth hundreds. Kathleen, who is still doing a bit of modelling and her husband, Leslie, will soon be celebrating their diamond wedding.

The scene of devastation after the disastrous fire at the Devon Pottery in 1951 which destroyed more than 44,000 square feet of the works. More than 400 dinner sets waiting to be packed for export were destroyed. It was nearly six months before Fieldings got back into production and it was the end of 1954 before the factory got into full output again. Although Fieldings took over the rival fancyware manufactuer Shorter and Sons in 1964, many believe that the great fire was the beginning of the end. The Fielding connection ended in 1967 when the managing director Reg Fielding retired.

Crown Devon for sale at the South African specialist ceramic store of Cleghorn and Harris who also arranged an exhibition of Crown Devon wares in 1939

at a Crown Devon exhibition in a large store. She had escaped with her baby daughter on the last ship out of Hong Kong when the Japanese invaded and had to leave her husband behind. He was taken prisoner and she didn't hear from him for more than two years.

Before she married and went to live in the Far East with her husband Leslie, Kathleen modelled a series of dog head studies for Crown Devon. They sold for 10 shillings (50p)/$0.90 and today they fetch between £90/$175 and £120/$230. But the art deco figurines are worth much more. Priced at between 10 shillings (50p)/$0.90 and £1/$1.80 they now have an asking price of anything between £300/$550 and £600/$1150.

Success continued at Sutherland Street after the war under the direction of the last Managing Director Reg Fielding, but the Great Fire of May 16th 1951 was probably the beginning of the end of a company which produced a century of ceramics which the people of the Potteries were proud to call their own.

The Fielding connection ended in 1967 and the pottery finally closed in 1982 but now Crown Devon products are sought after more than they have ever been!

Backstamps

The word 'Fielding' impressed from 1878.
The initial letters 'S.F. & Co' were used on several printed marks from the late 1880s until after 1914-18 war. The name of the individual pattern was frequently included.
The ribbon mark with the letters 'S.F. & Co.' was used in the early 1880s.

The circular Crown Devon backstamp was used from the mid-eighties to the end of the decade.

  Printed marks from 1891 until the turn of the century.

The large Victorian crown with the letters 'S.F. & Co' was used from c1900 to c1910.

  Left: Four examples of printed marks which were used from c1910 to c1930.

  Right: This mark was introduced in 1930 and lasted with slight variations until well after the Second World War

 This mark was introduced in the Fifties and lasted with slight variations until the firm closed down.

The final backstamp with the words 'potters for over 100 years'.

The Mystery of Majolica

When Simon Fielding put money into the Railway Works in the 1870s, it was run by Hackney Kirkham and Company and one of the main products was majolica ware, which was very popular at that time. When Abraham Fielding took over some 18 months later he placed particular emphasis on majolica ware which was produced not only for the home market but for export as well.

In 1883, the *Ceramic Art of Great Britain* by Llewellyn Jewitt stated that 'The Railway Pottery', Sutherland Street, Stoke-on-Trent, was established by S Fielding and Co in 1878 for the manufacture of Majolica, Terracotta, Jet, Rockingham and green-glazed fancy goods and general earthenware, in all which the useful, ornamental and fancy articles are made. The mark of the firm is a gamecock.

On page 626 of the same book he states, 'One of the distinctive features of the majolica produced by S. Fielding and Co is the masterly and effective way in which they introduce hand-modelled flowers and foliage to some of their best pieces. Modelled and coloured true to nature in every minute detail and thrown in graceful negligence around the bodies of the vases, they become such perfect reproductions that it is difficult to divest the mind of the idea that the roses are not freshly gathered from the tree and temporarily wound round the vase for its adornment'.

One of these vases, some two feet or more in height, is one of the highest achievements in this phase of the plastic art. The double handles on either side are formed of branches of the rose tree cut from its parent stem and elegantly arched to form the leaves, the buds and the full-blown roses. Every petal is exquisitely modelled by hand and gracefully and naturally arranged.

'The cover, in keeping with the general idea of the design, is a robin which serves as a handle, in a bed of roses'. The article states that majolica had been the company's staple trade and the company mark was Fielding impressed or the name on a ribbon with the initials S.F and Co.

There is no doubt that the popularity of majolica waned in the late 1880s and Fielding switched to other wares but of the majolica produced at Railway Works between 1878 and 1890, little appears to have survived. If it has, then little of it comes on to the open market. Majolica seems to be increasing in popularity. I have seen one or two pieces of George Jones majolica and read about several others at auction and all have fetched high prices. But Fieldings' majolica is much of a mystery. I have spoken to dealers who say they have had one or two pieces over the years but I have never been offered a piece with the Fielding or Railway Works mark.

However, there are plenty of Fieldings pieces around which date from the last decade of the 19th century to prove that the company produced a wide range of fancy goods which included vases, sardine dishes, butter dishes and biscuit jars.

An advert in the *Pottery Gazette* of 1897 showed a selection of ornamental wares. Very popular were the jug and bowl toilet sets which today fetch £250 or more, cheese dishes, jugs, flower pots, biscuit jars, dessert sets, salad and punch bowls and of course, teapots. Also advertised were china tea services with pattern names such as Clifton, Dee, Jersey, May, Marigold and Turin. Some of these have survived and are fine examples of china ware.

FOOTNOTE: Just before Christmas 1996, the phone rang and I thought it was Santa Claus when he said, "I have found three pieces of majolica made by Fieldings". On a trip to Toronto, he had spotted a sardine dish at £425, a jug about 5" high at £225 and a small plate at £110. Did he bring me one back? He thought they were too expensive! Two of the pieces had the Fieldings impressed mark and the diamond date stamp.

Nineteenth Century Products

Here are a few examples of nineteeth century work at the Fielding factory. Some were produced up to and beyond the turn of the century.

Wall plaque of Trentham Hall. BS: Impressed Fieldings, Stoke-on-Trent. Also the words 'With the compliments of Fieldings, Railway Works, Stoke-on-Trent, England', and the date 1893. On the front of the plaque are the words 'Trentham Hall, the seat of His Grace the Duke of Sutherland'. Size: 18 by 15 inches. PG: £500-£600/$950-$1100. Rare. Note. Other plaques carry scenes of Haddon Hall and Alton Towers and they were made between 1890 and 1910. Haddon Hall plaque No. 8 was dated 1902 and Haddon Hall plaque No. 32 was dated 1908.

Game dish in Royal Devon. BS: Large crown. PN: X369 Royal Devon. Size: 10 inches by 8. PG: £65-£75/$120-$140. Rare.

Game dish in Bon. BS: Large crown with datestamp 1897. PN: 03 Bon. Size: 10 inches by 8. PG: £75-£95/$150-$200.

Sugar caster with floral decoration. BS: Large crown. PN: X332. Artist's initial F. PG: £40-£45/$75-$85.

China cups and saucers and jug in Jersey pattern. BS: Crown on shield. RN: 186839 circa 1892. PN: C5. PG: £25-£35/$40-$70. Note. This tableware in bone china was produced in a full service to accommodate 12 people. A half service in good condition including milk jug and sugar basin and bread and butter plate would probably fetch around £200/$350. A teapot would add a further £60-£70/$110-$125. The teapots are rare.

Sardine dish in pink and blue. BS: Large crown in blue. PN: 373. PG: £50-£60/$90-$120. Rare.

Tobacco jar in Royal Kew. BS: Lion on crown S F and Co. PN: A33. Height: 6½ inches. PG: £75-£90/$140-$275. Rare.

Miniature flower pots. Left. Royal Lorne pattern. BS: Lion on crown S F and Co. PN: A24. PG: £50-£60/$90-$115. Right: Royal Persian pattern. BS: Lion on crown S F and Co. PN: X76. PG: £70-£80/$130-$150. Rare.

Oval dish in Rye pattern. BS: Crown on shield S F and Co. PN: 290 Rye. Size: 15 inches by 9. PG: £30-£40/$55-$75.

Tea kettle with gold leaf decoration. BS: Circular mark with small crown inset and four small stars. PN.73: RN: 108130, c1888. PG: £75-£85/$140-$175. Rare.

Game dish in Oxon. BS: Large crown. PN: X511. SN. Impressed 82. PG: £90-£100/$175-$200.

Sardine dish in Haddon. BS: Crown on shield. PN: X133.
PG: £45-£55/$80-$110.

Tobacco jar with gold leaf decoration.
BS: Circular mark with S F and Co.
above and small crown in centre. The
words 'Crown Devon' within the
outer circle. 1880s. PG: £75-
£85/$130-$160. Rare.

Hanging vase with original chain. BS: Lion on
crown. PN: Royal Clarence. RN: 205238 c.1892.
Height: 7 inches. PG: £70-£80/$130-$150.

China cup and saucer, milk jug and sugar basin in May. BS:
Crown on shield S F and Co. PN: C1 May c1891. PG: £35-
£45/$65-$90.

Royal Devon match striker. BS:
Fieldings impressed. PN: Royal
Devon. Marked Made for Cantrell
and Cochrane, Dublin and Belfast.
PG: £75-£85/$140-$160. Rare.

Beakers in Royal Sussex. BS: Lion on Crown S F and Co. PN: A18. Height
4 inches. PG: £40/$75 each. Rare.

15

Pair of Indian vases. BS: Ribbon mark S F and Co. PN: 625. SN impressed 52. Height: 10 inches. PG: £200-£250/$375-$475. *Rare.* Note. The Indian pattern was registered on 26th January 1882 with the diamond registration number of 376443.

Cup and saucer in Indian pattern. BS: Ribbon mark S F and Co. PN: 625. PG: £35-£45/$65-$80.

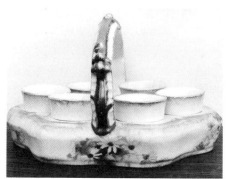

Bowl in Kent pattern. BS: Crown on shield S F and Co. RN: 15--63 (1890). PN: 843. PG: £50-£60/$90-$115. *Rare.* Note. The Kent pattern appeared again in 1910 with a registration number of 600413 and with a vastly different design. It was then renamed Lune with a pattern number of 0710.

Egg nest in Royal Lorne. BS: Lion on crown S F and Co. early 1890s. PN: A24. Royal Lorne. PG: £95-£105/$180-$200 with six egg cups undamaged.

Tea set in Clifton pattern. BS: Crown on shield. PN: C50. PG: 21-piece tea service £200/$375.

Biscuit barrel in Jap pattern. BS: Large crown S F and Co. PN: X822. Height: 6 inches. PG: £60-£75/$115-$140. *Rare.*

Fine examples of the vellum range for which Crown Devon is famous. Back: Wild Roses ewer, large Elm pattern vase, one of a pair at £300-£350/$550-$675, hors d'oeuvre dish in Spring, £80-£100/$150-$195. Front: candlestick in Etna, £25/$50, vase in Don, £75/$140, teapot in Royal Essex, £150-£200/$290-$395 with stand, Erin tankard, one of a pair, £150/$290.

More vellum. Back: Vase in Spring, rare shape, £75/$160, Crown Devon pattern jug, £100/$200, with a bowl, £225, Don pattern plate, £35-£45/$70-$90. Front: Unusual three-legged bowl in May, £80-£90/$150-$195, Royal Lorne jug, £25/$50, two-handled tankard in Teck, £90/$175, small Wick dish, $£25/45.

Two nineteenth century plates, £35-£45/$65-$90 each, a biscuit jar in Royal Sussex, quite rare, £125/$250, pair of Windsor vases, £70/$140.

Back: Royal Devon is the most expensive vellum and back left is an unusual vase, one of a pair worth £300/$475 followed by an earlier Royal Devon vase and one of a pair worth £150-£200/$295-$400. On the right a Thames hors d'hoevre dish, £80-£100/$150-$195. Front: early tea kettle in Cam, £75-£95/$140-$190, powder bowl, £30/$55, jug in Royal Stuart, £75-£85/$140-$170.

Nineteenth century teapot and stand in Jersey pattern, £70-£80/$135-$155.

Rare Royal Devon teapot, £100-£120/$190-$230.

Here are four examples of Crown Devon ware which are not easy to find. Good hunting!

An epergne in Salop pattern with silver-plated stand,
£200/$395.

One of a pair of Royal Chelsea vases worth between
£500-£600/$975-$1200.

Thames pattern condiment set to grace any table,
£75-£85/$140-$170.

Rare Royal Devon, an egg server, £65/$125 and match
striker £70/$135.

Part of a nineteenth century tea service in Wem. A perfect half service would command over £300/$600.

Part of a nineteenth century china tea service in Jersey pattern. Full 12-setting service with teapot £400/$800.

A pair of Indian vases often seen with a diamond registration mark, worth about £250/$500. The biscuit jar is in Derby pattern and is quite rare – must be worth around £100/$225.

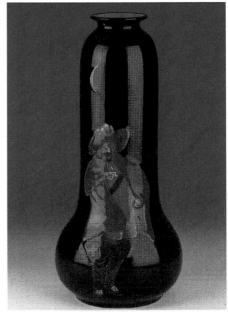

One of the rarest pieces I have seen, a glazed Toby jug incised Fieldings on the base. Hard to value – probably around £150/$290.

Another rare piece, a Royal Guelph vase which is impressed 'Royal Guelph' on the base. Worth £70-£80/$140-$160? Could be twice that!

Four examples of Crown Devon commemorative ware which sell for between £30/$55 and £90/$175. The biscuit-ground pieces fetch 50 per cent more than the ivory-ground.

Another selection of commemoratives. The George and Mary coronation paperweight is quite rare. So is the small plate.

This handsome jug in Mattajade is nearly 14 inches high and carries the Golden Dragon pattern. Several of the best Crown Devon art deco vases have topped £400/$795 in recent months and this would be no exception.

More Art Deco ware – and more and more Crown Devon collectors are seeking specimens such as the seat prices between £250/$495 and £300/$600.

More of the fascinating patterns in Crown Devon Art Deco ware at prices between £100/$190 and £150/$300.

Fifteen inch high vase in pattern M 391 and signed with the initial A.C. Price range £250-£300/$495-$600.

The ruby lustrine Temple jar is worth around £300-£350/$595-$700. The Pegasus piece around £50/$95 and the blue lustrine cigarette lighter the same amount.

The Mattajade candlestick and the pot pourri in design M162 are much more collectable than the two blue bird vases.

This Temple jar, was made by Fieldings in the 1920s. The pattern name is Chintz (number L 54B). Price: £350-£400/$700-$800.

Two rare handpainted vases on a black ground with pattern name 'Tokio' and number 0984. The price: £150/$295 the pair.

Here is a small lustrine dish with a Mavis bird pattern on a black ground. It is worth about £30/$55.

Here is one of a pair of Royal Khaki vases, believed to be Boer War mementoes, and worth about £100/$220.

Here are half a dozen of Fieldings' Ivrine series from left to right front: John Bull, £250-£300/$475-$600; Flower Girl £200-£250/$375-$500; Bulldog, and Stork flower holder £175-£350/$350-$700. The Water Carrier Figure on the right at the back is valued at £350-£400/$700-$800.

More Ivrine figures. From left to right: Retriever £200-£250/$375-$500; Madame Pompadour, Gainsboro Girl £250/$475; Girl in semi nude post £350-£400/$675-$800; and Tiger which is extremely rare

The cockerel vase on the left £200/$375, can be collected as a pair – that's if you can find one looking right and one looking left! The Elephant is worth about £300-£350/$575-$700.

Here is the coloured version of the Ivrine Madam Pompadour. She is ravishing and rare.

The Fruit Gatherer doesn't come cheap either. She'll grace any sideboard for between £350/$690 and £400/$820.

This pheasant is a much rarer bird than the live variety! You won't find many under £300/$600.

Here is a coloured version of Vanity. Very rare and quite expensive at around £375/$750.

Rio Rita, the best-known figure by Kathleen Parsons. One or two of Kathleen's figures are now nearing four figures.

Another outstanding figure by Kathleen Parsons and one which would fetch £400/$800 plus.

Figures by Kathleen Parsons with delightful names such as 'Dancing Waves' and 'Sea Treasures'. Prices start at £250/$500.

Kathleen Fisher models in the Sutherland cellulose range. In good condition they fetch more than £100/$190.

More Sutherland figures from the left: Marina, Patricia, Priscilla and Denise.

Five young ladies in the Sutherland underglaze. They are worth more than twice as much as their cellulose counterparts.

This picture shows how the celluose figures might have looked if they had been better painted!! They have the initials I.B. on the base and they are not for sale!

Here is Sutherland girl Patricia on a lamp whicih would have cost 26s 6d ($2.60). Today it would cost 200 times that

A small Rio Rita on a mirrored piece called Maytime. It cost 13s 6d/$1.25 in the Thirties. Around £200/$400 or more now.

Here are two young ladies produced in the early Twenties. They have backstamps of Fieldings 45 and 46 and in auction would probably fetch around £300/$580 each.

The Tyrolean peasant girl by Austrian Olga (Clare) Hartzeg. Princess Margaret was so impressed she bought one.

Another Hartzeg creation, the Russian Lady and Borzoi which has doubled in price in three years. The last one I saw for sale had an asking price of £770/$1550!!

The Beach Girl, again from the Hartzeg studio. You won't get much change, if any, out of £500/£1000.

Poor man's Worcester? Not any more. The handpainted pieces have escalated in price. These examples are by Hinton. The framed painting around £700/$1350, the vase £400/$825 plus.

Fruit plaque by Lamanby, vase by Harper and dish by Cole and you can start the bidding at £400/$795 for any of them.

Pheasants by Coleman, Cranes by Marsh and Peacocks by Stuart. This little trio would set you back close on £1000/$2000.

Painted by Cox, three delightful pieces which would enahnce any collection. The cabinet plates change hands at £250/$500 each.

Rose pieces are harder to find than most. The large vase would be £300-£350/$590-$700, the smaller pieces around £150/$300 each.

Here's a nice trio in Cranes by Marsh with a pair of cabinet plates and a charming centrepiece. About £750/$1500.

The framed ceramic plaques by chief artist Walter Lamonby and his staff get top marks in the collecting field. Here is one of Walter's Dogs and Pheasants.

And here are Highland cattle superbly painted by George Cox. Dogs may come top o' the pile but cattle run them a close second.

Musical novelties of the Thirties were popular then and are even more so today. From the left: Harry Lauder jug, the Eton Boating Song and the George VI and Queen Elizabeth Super jug. Worth £200/$350 each.

Three of the more common jugs, Killarney, Auld Lang Syne and Daisy Bell. They are not cheap but they look it compared to a Sandy Powell musical mug which sold in 1996 for £650/$1275.

The musical dog kennel cigarette box. Choice of three tunes, and favourite with young and old. Price £250-£300/$495-$590.

The Churchill bulldog – a favourite with everyone. One of three wartime souvenirs. Quite rare, about £275/$525.

Woeful Willy and Perky Pup, made in various sizes costing from £25/$45 to more than £100/$190.

Three of the champion dogs head studies by Kathleen Parsons. The alsatian is one of the most expensive at around £125/$250.

Two of a series of wall figures, the Russian Lady and the Hiker, modelled by Kathleen Parsons. From £150-£200/$275-$400.

This Fieldings clock in Royal Lorne pattern has two matching vases which makes it rather unique. Few Fielding clocks have survived. The trio would fetch £750/$1450.

This clock in the old Banff pattern has the original movement by the British United Clock Company. It should certainly be insured for £1000/$1950.

. . . *and finally a tip for 1997*

A collection of post-war decorative ware handpainted by Tom Wilcox and his fellow artists and named 'Devon Glory' and 'Lady Hamilton'. The smaller pieces can be picked up for as little as £40/$75. Don't miss them.

Art Deco

Many people regard the Art Deco period of the late Twenties and early Thirties as Crown Devon's finest hour. Expert Pat Watson recently wrote 'Few firms in the Potteries could equal Crown Devon in its heyday . . . high quality lustre vases, salad ware, novelty cruets, musical jugs and mugs, figurines and vivid Art Deco handpainted patterns. Crown Devon had them all'.

Here are a few examples of Fieldings' high quality Art Deco work. It isn't easy to find and it's quite expensive.

Mattajade dragon jug. BS: Thirties mark in gold. PN: 2319. Height: 14 inches. PG: £350-£400/$750-$800.

Dragon design candlestick and vase. BS: Thirties gold. PN: 2068. Height: Candlestick 9 inches, vase 8 inches. PG: Candlestick £60-£80/$115-$150, vase £150-£200/$290-$395.

Boxed coffee set in green and gold. Six cups and saucers and six gilt coffee spoons. BS: Thirties gold. PN: 2331. PG: £250-£300/$500-$600.

Boxed green and white bridge set. Four cups and saucers, a cigarette box and two ashtrays. BS: Thirties stamp in black. PN: 3022. PG: £350-£400/$690-$795.

Here are some popular Crown Devon Art Deco patterns which continue to fetch high prices.

AZTEC . . . a decorative border of zig-zags with fish.
ESPANOL . . . vivid borders in yellow, green, brown and purple.
MORESQUE . . . strips in Islamic blue.
MATTAJADE . . . stylised florals often with oriental influence i.e. Chinese dragon pattern M162.
MATTASUNG . . . spider pattern with dragonflies. M72.
FAIRY CASTLE . . . floral design in blue, green and gold with pale blue background. M34.
RUSTIC LUSTRINE . . . blue with enamel decoration.

Mattatone vase. BS: Thirties gold. PN: M118(A). SN: 367 7 inches. PG: £100-£120/$180-$230.

A collection of Art Deco ware which anyone would be proud to own.

Mattajade pot pourri and vase. BS: Thirties gold. PN: M162. Height. Pot pourri 6 inches, vase 6¹/₂ inches. PG: £100-£120/$180-$230 each.

Pair of rare pink and gold vases. BSL: Thirties gold. PN: 0174. SN: 216 4¹/₂ inches. PG: £100/$185 the pair.

Fairy Castle jug. BS: Thirties gold. PN: M264. SN: 349. 6 inches. PG: £250-£300/$475-$600.

Mattasung vase with cover. BS: Thirties gold. PN: M72. Height: 7¹/₂ inches. PG: £120-£150/$230-$290.

The Crown Devon lustrine series was introduced in the early Twenties when lustre ware became popular at the luxury end of the market. Here are some examples of the ware that continued for more than a decade.

  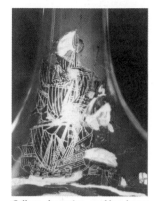

Temple jar in ruby lustre. BS: Thirties gold. Height: 15½ inches. PG: £300-£325/$595-$650.

Rare jar in blue with gold leaf decoration. BS: L54B – Chintz. Height: 16 inches. PG: £350-£400/$690-$800.

Galleon decoration on blue lustre vase. BS: Thirties gold. PG: £50-£60/$90-$115.

Left: Ruby lustre vase with pearline interior. BS: Thirties gold. PN: 2979. Height: 5½ inches. PG: £55/$100. Right: Attractive bird pattern jug in royal blue. BS: Thirties gold. SN: EI07SS. PG: £80/$150.

Galleon wall plaque in a rich assortment of colour. BS: Thirties gold. PN: M169. Diameter: 12 inches PG: £200-£250/$375-$500.

Rare mermaid and fish pattern in green. BS: Twenties small crown in black. PN: L4. SN: 130 Height: 12 inches. PG: £100-£125/$190-$240.

Pair lustre vases with blue and gilt butterfly decoration. BS: Twenties small crown in gold with Devon Lustrine above. PN: L52. SN: 131 Height: 9 inches. PG: £100-£125/$190-$250.

Handsome Art Deco jug and vase. BS: Thirties gold. PG: £150-£200/$280-$400 the pair.

Pair unusual blue lustre vases with floral decoration. BS: Thirties gold. PN: M2. PG: £125-£150/$240-$300.

Ruby lustre basket and jug in gold leaf decoration. BS: Thirties gold. PN: S293. SN: Basket A150, jug A534. PG: Both pieces £60-£75/$115-$150 each.

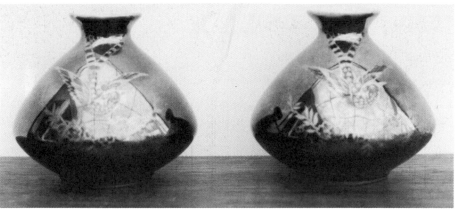

Pair 3 inch blue lustre vases with bird decoration. BS: Twenties small crown in gold. PN: L70. SN: 46. Height: 3 inches. PG: £45-£50/$85-$95.

Art Deco lamp (shade not original). BS: Thirties backstamp. SN: 708. PG: £60-£75/$115-$150.

Unusual pair of pale blue lustrine vases. BS: Small crown. PN: 28 Birch. Height: 6 inches. PG: £75-£95/$140-$200.

Left: Devon lustrine vase with bird decoration on blue background. BS: Twenties small crown in gold. PN: L70. PG: £65-£85/$120-$150.
Right: Rare orange lustre vase with four flying birds and background in black against orange sky. BS: Twenties small crown in black with Devon ware above. PN: L63. SN: 131 Height: 9 inches. PG: £75-£95/$140-$200.

1890-1900 . . . Vellum leads the way

This was the decade that set Abraham Fielding on the road to success. He introduced new techniques, new ovens, in fact all the working requirements of a modern earthenware factory. In 1892 a whole row of cottages came down in Sutherland Street and gave way to new ovens, a warehouse, printing and painting shops followed by a glaze mill. Records show that at that time the company introduced a vellum ware which was to become the best-selling product from the Railway works for more than 20 years.

Many Crown Devon collectors want nothing else but vellum ware. It was produced in a huge variety of patterns with both ivory and cream grounds and it is the cream ware which is so popular today.

When did Fieldings introduce the name 'Crown Devon' to its wares? This has been the subject of debate for years but there is no doubt that Crown Devon appeared on a variety of patterns on vellum ware in the early 1890s.

There is no doubt, too, that the name 'Royal Devon' appeared on several patterns during the same period and during that time between 1890 and 1895 a number of other 'Royals' arrived including Royal Chelsea (there was a Crown Chelsea, too), Royal Sussex, Royal Clarence and Royal Essex. In the second half of the decade came such favourites as Royal York, Royal Tudor, Royal Persian, Royal Khaki, Royal Eton, Royal Kent and Royal Suffolk. At the turn of the century, the name 'Royal Devon' continued to appear on a variety of patterns. I have seen it on a game dish with a large white flower spray and green surround and pattern number X369. I have seen it on a pair of vases with the Royal Devon spray edged in blue and pattern number X392. I have seen it on a chamber pot with large purple flowers and pattern number 025.

It has appeared on a shell vase with a medallion pattern and pattern number X962. All these pieces had large crown backstamps. The shell vase had a registration number RN: 348898 – the only registration number I have seen on a piece marked 'Royal Devon'.

The Royal Devon design that established itself in the early days was the orange and green spray (pattern number X712) but the Royal Devon design that took over was the white Rhodesian rose tinged with red and bordered by small blue flowers. This design carried a large crown backstamp and pattern number X543.

Royal Chelsea was the most expensive of the royals and there were various decorations featuring a shaded matt ground in different combinations of colours with floral sprays traced in gold.

Royal Wisterian had a similar decoration in the early days when it was believed to have been aimed at the North American market but details in the pattern books which have survived are very sparse and in some cases rather contradictory.

Following the success of the royals, Fieldings introduced scores of new patterns in the vellum range mostly with a cream matt ground.

Royal Chelsea - one of a pair circa 1890s. BS: Crown on shield. PN: 19. SN: 95. Height: 15¹/₂ inches. PG: £500-£600/$950-$1200 the pair.

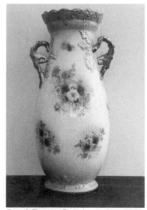

Royal Devon floor vase circa 1900. BS: Large crown. PN: 543. SN: 122. Height: 22 inches (one of a pair). PG: £750/$1500 the pair.

Golden Poppy pattern circa 1884. BS: None. RN: 145015. Height: 9 inches. PG: £150-£175/$275-$350 the pair.

Etna pattern urn with cover circa 1910. BS: Small crown. PN: 0623. RN: 578617. Height: 26 inches. PG: £600/$1150.

Spring pattern vase. One of a pair circa 1912. BS: Small crown. PN: 1000. RN: 653216. Height: 12 inches. PG: £300/$625 the pair.

Royal Sussex vases circa 1895. BS: Lion on crown. PN: A18. SN: 27. Height: 10 inches. PG: £175-£200/$330-$400.

Thames pattern vase circa 1912. BS: Small crown. PN: 1025. RN: 658051. Height: 13½ inches. PG: £100/$190.

Pair of chimney vases in Royal Devon. BS: Large crown. PN: X543. SN: 16. Height: 11½ inches. PG: £175-£200/$350-$400.

Many were named after rivers such as Avon, Clyde, Esk, Lune, Trent, Thames and Wye.

Place names were popular, too. There were Aden, Banff, Bonn, Chester, Ely, Erin, Filey, Leeds, Nankin, Oxon, Pekin, Perth, Riga, Ripon, Rye, Salop, Wem, Wick and many, many more.

Other favourites were Festoon, Gem, Pendant, Ribbon, Teck and we must not forget Spring which is the second most desirable pattern in the vellum range after Royal Devon.

Vellum range in vases

The Vellum range has proved to be the most collectable during the past decade and good examples are getting harder to find. The most popular pattern is Royal Devon (pattern number X543) although pattern X712 isn't far behind. Other popular royals are Royal Sussex and Royal Stuart but patterns such as Spring, Wick, Teck, Banff, Salop and Perth are as popular now as they were 80 or more years ago.

Pair unusual shape vases in Spring. BS: Small crown. PN: 1000. RN: 653216. Height: 10 inches. PG: £150-£175/$300-$350.

Pair Don pattern vases circa 1910. BS: Small crown. RN: 602047. PN: 1076. Height: 11 inches. PG: £150-£175/$275-$325.

Eva pattern vases with covers. BS: Small crown. PN: 0941. RN: 651328. Height: (including covers) 10 inches. PG: £250-£275/$475-$350.

Pair of Royal Essex vases. BS: Lion on crown. PN: 998. SN: 84. Height: 8½ inches. PG: £80-£90/$150-$180.

Left: Esk pattern. BS: Small crown. PN: 1021. RN: 607585. SN: 64. Height: 10 inches. PG: £60/$115. Right: Royal Clarence c1893. BS: Lion on crown. PN: 823. SN: 9. Height: 9 inches. PG: £60/$115.

Two vases in Wick pattern circa 1912. BS: Small crown. PN: 0992. SN: 39. RN: 548631. Height: 9½ inches with covers. PG: £250-£275/$475-$550.

Unusual vase in Royal Devon – one of a pair. BS: Large crown. PN: X543. SN: 16. Height: 11½ inches. PG: £250-£300/$475-$590 the pair.

Vase and cover in Dora. BS: Small crown, Crown Devon, Fieldings. RN: 629323. Height: 10 inches with cover. PN: 0871 circa 1911. PG: £125-£150/$225-$300.

Left: Crown Devon serpent vase circa 1890s. BS: Lion on crown. PN: 0112. SN: 40. Height: 11 inches. PG: £75-£100/$140-$200. Right: Royal York vase 1890s. BS: Crown on shield. SN: 66. Height: 13 inches. PG: £50-£60/$90-$175.

Pair of small Windsor vases. BS: Small crown. PN: 0804. SN: 43. Height: 6½ inches. PG: £55-£65/$100-$120.

Spring vases – the second most popular pattern. BS: Small crown. PN: 1000 circa 1912. RN: 653216. Height: 10 inches. PG: £150-£175/$275-$350.

Pair of Royal Chelsea vases. BS: Crown on shield S F and Co. PN: 14/3. Height: 11 inches. PG: £250-£275/$475-$550. Rare.

Left: Royal Scotia vase. BS: Lion in crown S F and Co. PN: 985. Height: 8 inches. PG: £100-£125/$190-$250. Rare. Right: Royal Essex vase. BS: Lion on crown S F and Co. PN: 998. Height: 8 inches. PG: £60-£75/$110-$150.

Two miniature vases in Banff. BS: Small crown Crown Devon S F and Co. RN: 517393. SN: 8. PN: 0596. Height: 6 inches. PG: £150-£175/$290-$350.

Pair of Royal Windsor vases. BS: Crown on shield S F and Co. PN: 851. Height: 9½ inches. PG: £100-£125/$195-$250. Note: This pattern is also known as Chrysanthemum.

One of a pair of Elm vases. BS: Crown on shield S F and Co. PN: X69. SN: 57. Height: 14 inches. PG: £200-£250/$375-$500. Rare.

Chimney vase in Rye. BS: Crown on shield S F and Co. SN: 16. Height: 11 inches. PG: £70-£100/$130-$195.

Early Royal Lorne vase. BS: Lion on crown. PN: A24. Height: 10½ inches. PG: £100-£125/$190-$250. Rare.

Two handpainted vases with pattern name 'Tokio' and number 0984. The Japanese lady dominates a mythical scene. Price: £150/$275.

Aden pattern vases. BS: Large crown circa 1904. PN: X786. Height: 9 inches. PG: £125-£150/$230-$290.

Eva pattern with covers – one of a pair. BS: Small crown. PN: 0941. RN: 651328. Height: 16½ inches including covers. PG: £300-£350/$575-$650 the pair.

Left: Metz pattern in ivory. BS: Crown on shield. PN: 134. SN: 54. Height: 8½ inches. PG: £30/$50. Note. Some of the vases of this period were finished in ivory. These are not as popular with collectors hence the reflection in the price. Right: Royal Sussex vase. BS: Lion on crown. PN: A18. SN: 89. PG: £75-£90/$140-$175.

Unusual shape vase in Crown Devon pattern. BS: Lion on crown. PN: Crown Devon. SN: 101. Height: 10½ inches. PG: £75-£100/$135-$200.

Miniature vase or posy bowl. BS: Large crown, S F and Co., England. PN: X543 Royal Devon. Height: 3 inches. PG: £40-£50/$75-$95. Rare.

Art Nouveau ewer in Royal Chelsea. BS: Crown on shield S F and Co. PN: 14/2. Height: 13 inches. PG: £125-£150/$240-$450. Rare.

The Royals, their dates, and their backstamps

1891 Royal Chelsea (crown on shield). Several patterns lined in gold
Royal Devon (circular mark with a variety of patterns).

1892 Royal Clarence (lion on crown).
Royal Essex (lion on crown).
Royal Sussex (lion on crown).

1893 Royal Lorne (lion on crown).
Royal Stuart (lion on crown).
Royal Kew (lion on crown).

1894 Royal Scotia (lion on crown).

1895 Royal York (crown on shield).
Royal Kent (crown on shield).

1896 Royal Eton (crown on shield).

1898 Royal Suffolk (lion on crown).

1899 Royal Windsor (lion on crown).
Royal Oxford (lion on crown).
Royal Tudor (lion on crown).
Royal Persian (lion on crown).

1900 Royal Khaki (lion on crown).
Royal Wisterian (crown on shield).

1902 Royal Devon pink and white (large crown) X543.

1904 Royal Devon orange and green (large crown). This pattern also appeared in the late 1890s with a Crown Devon mark and a lion on crown backstamp.

1907 Royal Pearl (large crown).

Threesome in Clyde pattern: BS: Large crown S F and Co. PN: X380. Height: 9 inches. PG: £50-£70/$90-$130 for each vase.

Two shapes in Royal York. BS: Crown on shield S F and Co. Left: SN: 50. Right: SN: 28. PG: £60-£80/$110-$160 each.

Three other royals were introduced. Royal Osborne (1902), Royal Delft (1903) and Royal Guelph (1910) but they were entirely different to the vellum royals and none of them was made in any numbers and examples are few are far between. Despite their rarity they are not favourites with collectors.

The Royals

Royal Chelsea – pink and primrose flowers lined in gold with pink and light blue leaves. No pattern number. This is just one of several Royal Chelsea patterns. Very rare, very collectable.

Royal Clarence – pattern 996 – purple and yellow flowers with green and brown leaves on a cream background shaded to fawn at the edges and tipped with gold. Pattern number 823 or A23 – small red and blue flowers with larger pale green leaves on a vellum cream background. Design edged with bold gold border top and bottom.

Royal Devon – pattern numbers X369, X482, X712, X962 and 025-white and orange flowers on a background of green leaves blending into light fawn and edged in gold.

Royal Devon – pattern X543-white and pink or red flowers with green leaves and blue forget-me-nots against a cream background deepening to fawn and edged with gold.

Royal Essex – pattern 998-cream and purple chrysanthemum-style flowers on a cream

60

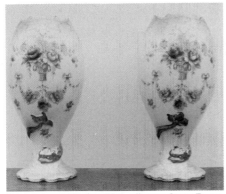

Serpent vases in Windsor. BS: Small crown Crown Devon, Fieldings. PN: 0799. Height: 11 inches. PG: £200-£250/$375-$750 the pair. Rare.

Two vases in shape No. 1081. Left: Royal Devon PN: X543. Right: Bon PN: M04. BS: Both large crown S F and Co. PG: £55-£75/$100-$140 each vase.

background blending to light blue, light green, light fawn or brown. Gold trim.

Royal Eton – pattern number 871-large sprays of carnations on cream background.

Royal Kew – pattern 993-yellow and grey pansy-type flowers with deeper yellow leaves against a glowing pink background blending to cream and fawn.

Royal Khaki – pattern X184-a commemorative royal with five-flag emblem and motto 'Dieu et mon droit'. Believed to be Boer War souvenir. The jugs and vases are in fawn with pink trim and pale pink interior. Edged with gold. Very rare.

Royal Lorne – pattern A24-yellow and pink flowers on a cream background deepening to light fawn. Gold trim.

Royal Oxford – pattern X94-purplish flower on a light green/fawn ground with gold border.

Royal Pearl – pattern 0193-purple old English roses with green leaves against a blush pink ground with gold edging.

Royal Persian – pattern X76-terracotta red flowers with gilt-edged leaves on a cream ground deepening to terracotta red above and below and edged in gold.

Royal Scotia – pattern 985-The Scottish thistle on a cream ground with colours of green, pink and mauve and trimmed with gold. Very rare.

Royal Stuart – pattern A28-small purple, pink and cream flowers on ivory ground with larger green leaves. Edged in gold.

Royal Stuart – pattern A29-small purple, pink and white flowers with green leaves on cream ground with blush pink shading.

Royal Suffolk – Purple and pink flowers on cream ground and trimmed in gold.

Royal Sussex – pattern A18-purple and pink peony-style flowers with gold decoration on a cream ground and edged in gold.

Royal Tudor – pattern X62-small deep red and yellow flowers on a deep cream ground and decorated and edged in gold.

Royal Windsor – pattern X51-chrysanthemum-style flowers in blue and fawn on a cream ground. Edged in gold and quite often with a high gloss glaze. This design is also known as 'Chrysanthemum'. A later pattern number was 0799.

Royal York – no pattern number-fuschia-style flowers in blue and cream with fawn leaves on both ivory and cream ground. Trimmed with gold. Also red and white flowers on yellow and blue ground.

Royal Wisterian – no pattern number-a floral spray sometimes lined in gold on a cream ground. Also produced with Wisterian-type flowers on a cream ground.

Note. In the absence of documentation, all the pattern numbers given for the royals have been taken from actual pieces over the years.

This jardiniere complete with stand turned up at Coventry last year with a most unusual poppy pattern. Carrying the Lion on Crown backstamp and pattern name Royal Clarence it is nothing like the Royal Clarence patterns of 996 and 823. With minor damage to a handle the price was right at around £900/$1800.

A pair of superb ewers 17 inches high with the rare Wild Roses pattern. The backstamp is Lion on Crown S F and Co, Stoke-on-Trent. The pattern name is Crown Devon and the number 0112 but registrations expert Frank Mason confirmed that 0112 was in fact Wild Roses. The vases are valued at £350/$700.

Indian Tree vases in blue. BS: Small crown Crown Devon, Fieldings. SN: 23. Height: 8½ inches. PG: £120-£150/$240-$280. Rare.

Pair of Royal Eton vases. BS: Large crown S F and Co. PN: 871. Height: 9 inches. PG: £120-£150/$230-$300.

Musicals Galore

Crown Devon launched the John Peel series of musical novelties in the early Thirties with a half-pint tankard, a pint tankard and a jug followed by a cigarette box, whisky flagon and salad bowl. These were followed by Widdicombe Fair (jug, two tankards and two cigarette boxes), on Ilkla Moor Baht 'at (jug, two tankards and two cigarette boxes), Auld Lang Syne (jug, two tankards and two cigarette boxes), Killarney (jug, two tankards and two cigarette boxes) and Daisy Bell (jug, two tankards and two cigarette boxes).

Left: John Peel half-pint tankard. BS: Crown Devon, Fieldings, Made in England printed on base. RN: 755780. Height. 5 inches. PG: £60-£80/$100-$150. Centre. John Peel pint tankard. BS: Crown Devon printed. RN: 755780. Height. 6 inches. PG: £80-£100. Right: John Peel jug. BS: Crown Devon printed. RN 755789. Height. 8 inches. PG: £100-£150/$190-$300.

Left: Widdicombe Fair half-pint tankard. BS: printed on base. RN: 804874. Height. 5 inches. PG: £65-£85/$120-$150. Centre. Widdicombe Fair pint tankard. BS: Printed on base. RN: 804874. Height. 6 inches. PG: £90-£110/$170-$210. Right: Widdicombe Fair jug. BS: Printed on base. RN: 802897. Height. 8 inches. PG: £120-£160/$225-$320.

Left: Auld Lang Syne half-pint tankard. BS: Printed on base. RN: 804873. Height. 5 inches. PG: £75-£95/$130-$230. Centre. Old Lang Syne pint tankard. BS: Printed on base. RN: 804873. Height. 6 inches. PG: £100-£110/$190-$200. Right: Old Lang Syne jug. BS: Printed on base. RN: 804875. Height. 8 inches. PG: £150-£200/$290-$600.

Left: Daisy Bell half-pint tankard. BS: Printed on base. RN: 812297. Height. 5 inches. PG: £80-£100/$150-$200. Centre. Daisy Bell pint tankard. BS: Printed on base. RN: 812297. Height. 6 inches. PG: £120-£140/$230-$275. Right: Daisy Bell jug. BS: Printed on base. RN: 812297. Height. 8 inches. PG: £200-£250/$380-$500.

Left: Ilkla Moor half-pint tankard. BS: Printed on base. RN: 807251. Height. 5 inches. PG: £75-£90/$140-$180. Centre: Ilkla Moor pint tankard. BS: Printed on base. RN: 807251. Height. 6 inches. PG: £100-£110/$200-$220. Right: Ilkla Moor jug. BS: Printed on base. RN: 807252. Height: 8 inches. PG: £130-£160/$250-$300.

Left: Killarney half-pint tankard. BS: Printed on base. RN: Applied for. Height: 5 inches. PG: £80-£100/$150-$200. Centre: Killarney pint tankard. BS: Printed on base. RN: Applied for. Height: 6 inches. PG: £100-£110/$190-$200. Right: Killarney jug. BS: Printed on base. RN: Applied for. Height: 8 inches. PG: £150-£200/$275-$375.

John Peel flagon. BS: Printed on base. RN: 796688. Height: 8 inches. PG: £175-£225/$330-$425.

Daisy Bell flagon. BS: Printed on base. RN: 812207. Height: 8 inches. PG: £250-£300/$500-$600.

The Gracie Fields jug. BS: Printed on base. Height: 8 inches. Music: Sally in our Alley. PG: £450-£500/$875-$1000.

Some of the jugs were also made in flat-bottom style without music. These included John Peel, Widdicombe Fair, Ilkla Moor, Auld Lang Syne, Killarney and Daisy Bell. Prices range from £65/$120 for John Peel to £150/$300 for Daisy Bell. Note. Several flat-bottom jugs including John Peel, Widdicombe Fair and the Eton Boating Song (a rare one) have been seen at fairs around the country this past few years. The writer is not convinced that all these were original products.

Edward VIII Coronation jug known as the abdication jug. Height: 8 inches. Tune. The National Anthem. PG. £450-£500/$900-$1000. Note. Some of the jugs had an alternative to the National Anthem. It was 'Here's a Health unto His Majesty'.

George VI and Queen Elizabeth Coronation jug. Height: 8 inches. Tune: The National Anthem. PG: £400-£450/$775-$900.

John Peel cigarette box. BS: Printed on the side, Crown Devon Made in England. RN: 813582. Music: John Peel. Size: 8 by 5 inches. PG: £300-£350/$575-$700. The Widdicombe Fair embossed cigarette box is very rare. The price: £500/$975 plus.

Highland cattle handpainted cigarette box. BS: Thirties stamp. PN: 0783. SN: 976. Painting signed by G. Cox. Tune: Ilkley Moor. PG: £200-£250/$375-$500.

Sir Harry Lauder jug. BS: Printed on base. Height: 8 inches. Music: I love a Lassie. PG: £350-£400/$675-$800.

Eton Boating Song jug. BS: Printed on base. Height: 8 inches. PG: £450-£500/$900-$1000.

The Ash Grove musical jug. BS: Printed on base. Height: 8 inches. PG: £400-£450/$775-$875.

The Sarais Marais series was made for South Africa and included a half-pint tankard (£225-£275/$425-$550) – they are rare – and a jug (£500-£550/$950-$1050).

Auction prices up

Footnote. At a specialist auction at Reading in March 1996, the following hammer prices were recorded (all musicals). Salad bowl and servers £550/$1050, Killarney pint tankard £160/$300, I love a Lassie pint tankard £160/$300, half-pint John Peel £70/$130, Sarais Marais pint tankard £300/$575, Sarais Marais jug £650/$1250. A very rare South African jug called Omdie Kampvuur (Around the camp fire) was knocked down for £700/$1350. These figures were well above those recorded in 1995.

Sarais Marais pint tankard. BS: Printed on base. Height: 6 inches. PG: £200-£250/$375-$500.

George VI Coronation musical cigarette box. PG: £250-£300/$475-$600.

George VI and Queen Elizabeth Coronation musical cigarette box. PG: £300-£350/$575-$700.

Left: George VI and Queen Elizabeth Coronation ashtray. PG: £30-£40/$50-$75. Right: George VI and Queen Elizabeth Coronation mug (musical). Tune: The National Anthem. PG: £80-£110/$150-$225.

John Peel musical cigarette box. BS: Thirties mark. SN: 4. Painting signed W. Lamonby. Size. 5½ by 3½ inches. Tune: John Peel. PG: £110-£140/$200-$300.

Olde England series musical cigarette box. BS: Thirties stamp in black. SN: 976. and called 'Warwick'. Tune: Goodnight Irene. PG: £70-£90/$130-$180.

Killarney musical cigarette box. PG: £300-£350/$575-$725.

Farewell with a University tankard

Oxford University half-pint tankard. BS: Crown Devon hand-written. No crown. PN: 2982 in gold. Height: 5 inches. Tune: Auld Lang Syne. PG: £100-£150/$180-$300. Rare. Note. Similar tankards were made for Cambridge University and Queen's University, Belfast. Many were used as farewell gifts to university people joining the Forces during the '39-45 war.

Crown Devon kennel cigarette box. Music plays 'The Whistler and his dog' or 'Daddy wouldn't buy me a bow-wow'. BS: Thirties mark in black. RN: Applied for. Size: 9 inches high, 5 inches wide and 5 inches deep. PG: £250-£300/$475-$600.

Robbie Burns Goblet (not musical). PG: £80-£100/$150-$190.

John Peel lamp (not musical). PG: With original shade. £150-£175/ $275-$340. Without original shade (as shown). £70-£80/$130-$150.

George VI and Queen Elizabeth Superjug. BS: Crown Devon musical coronation jug – limited edition of 1500. This jug is number 12 made by S Fielding and Co., Stoke-on-Trent, England. PG: £700-£800/$1300-$1575. Tune: The National Anthem.

New Zealand jug, with picture of Captain Cook's first landing. Tune: Now is the Hour. Height: 7½ inches. PG: £500-£600/$950-$1200.

Edward VIII Coronation Superjug. BS: Crown Devon musical coronation jug – limited edition of 1500. This jug is number 74 made by S Fielding and Co., Stoke-on-Trent, England. PG: £750-£800/$1400-$1575. Tune: The National Anthem, or Here's a Health unto His Majesty. Note. This jug is also known as the Abdication jug and jugs which carry the words 'Abdicated' and the date, fetch up to £1000/$1850.

Auld Lang Syne whisky flagon. PG: £250-£300/$465-$590.

Toby jug marked Charrington's. Height: 9 inches. Tune: Tavern in the Town. PG: £200-£250/$375-$475.

Daisy Bell musical cigarette box. PG: £300-£375/$575-$750.

John Peel biscuit barrel (not musical). PG: £80-£100/$150-$190.

Harry Lauder jug. Tune: Roamin' in the gloaming. PG: £250-£300/$490-$600.

Elizabeth II Coronation tankard 1953. Height: 5½ inches. Tune: The National Anthem. PG: £100-£150/$190-$300.

Small John Peel jug. Height. 6 inches. Tune. John Peel. PG: £80-£100/$150-$190.

Gracie Fields half-pint tankard. Tune. Sally in our Alley. Height: 5 inches. PG: £200-£250/$375-$500.

Harry Lauder half-pint tankard. Tune. I Love a Lassie. Height: 5 inches. PG: £120-£140/$230-$275.

John Peel musical bowl with fox handles. PG: £250-£300/$475-$600.

Edward VIII Coronation musical cigarette box. PG: £300-£350/$595-$700.

Ivrine Figures of the Twenties

Fieldings introduced the Ivrine series of figures – statuesque, animals and birds – in 1919 and production continued for more than a decade. These figures have always been quite rare and prices have escalated by more than 100 per cent during the past three years.

Left: The stork (produced as a pair, left and right). BS: Small crown. SN: Fieldings 3. PG: £175/$350. Right: The cockerel produced as a pair, left and right). BS: Small crown. Height: 11 inches. SN: Fieldings 4. PG: £200/$375. The cockerel comes with or without gilding on the vase.

Left: John Bull and his bulldog. BS: Small crown. SN: Fieldings 7. Height 12 inches. PG: £250-£300/$475-$600. Right: Madam Pompadour. This figure was also produced in colour and glazed. BS: Small crown. SN: Fieldings 11. Height: 13 inches. PG: £250-£300/$475-$600.

The first in the series was a retriever with a duck. The figure from nose to tail is 10 inches long and 5 inches high. The animal stands on a greenish base which is stamped with a small crown and 'Crown Devon Ivrine, Fieldings, Stoke-on-Trent'. BS: Small crown. SN: impressed Fieldings 1. PG: £200-£250/$400-$500.

Left: The Eagle. BS: Small crown. SN: Fieldings 36. Height: 8 inches. PG: £225-£275/$425-$575. Right: The Tawny Owl. BS: Small crown. SN: Fieldings 42. Height: 12 inches. PG: £225-£275/$425-$575.

The Gainsboro Girl – number 17 and worth around £250/$475.

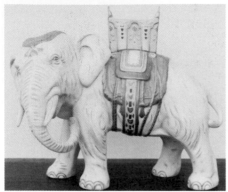

The elephant. BS: Small crown. SN: Fieldings 5. Height 10 inches. PG: With coloured decoration £300-£350/$575-$700. Without decoration £250-£300/$490-$600.

Classical Greek figures. BS: Small crown. Left: Lady with jar SN: Fieldings 14. Right: Lady with jar and flowers. SN: Fieldings 15. Height 13 inches. PG: £500-£550/$975-$1100 the pair.

Classical lady with fruit. BS: Small crown. SN: Fieldings 32. Height: 18 inches. PG: £350-£400/$700-$800. Rare.

Girl water carrier. BS: Small crown. SN: Fieldings 8. Height: 22 inches. PG: £350-£400/$700-$800. Rare.

The Jester. This figure is coloured and glazed and has not been seen in Ivrine. BS: Small crown. SN: Fieldings 53. Height 13 inches. PG: £350-£400/$695-$1400.

The Pheasant. BS: Small crown. SN: Fieldings 38. Height: 9 inches. Length 15 inches. PG: £250-£300/$500-$600.

Girl in semi-nude pose. BS: Small crown. SN: Fieldings 29. Height 15 inches. PG: £350-£400/$700-$800.

The Squirrel. This figure coloured and glazed has not been seen in Ivrine. BS: The words 'Crown Devon, Fieldings, England' handpainted in black. SN: 2224 (early Thirties). Height: 9 inches. PG: £125-£150/$230-$300.

Two budgies in green and yellow. This is another piece which is difficult to classify. Made in the Twenties it is finished in high glaze. BS: Small crown. Height: 9 inches. PG: £150-£200/$300-$400.

Flower girl in Bronzine. BS: Small crown. SN: Fieldings 12. Height: 12 inches. PG: £150-£175/$270-$325 in Bronzine, £200-£250/400-$500 in Ivrine. She is also known as Red Riding Hood.

Other figures I have seen in the Ivrine range are:

1914-18 War Officer preparing to 'go over the top'. A superb figure impressed Fieldings 9 with small crown backstamp. About 14 inches high and valued at £300-£350/$595-$700.

Gainsborough Girl – a figure 11 inches high and impressed Fieldings 17 with small crown backstamp. PG: £225-£275/$425-$550.

Newfoundland dog – a large and impressive piece with Fieldings 6 impressed on the base but carrying no backstamp. This was bought at Alexandra Palace in November 1995 for a very humble sum. The Fieldings mark was almost invisible and neither seller or buyer knew exactly what the figure was. Its value £300-£350/$575-$700.

The Fox – BS: Small crown. SN: Fieldings 10. PG: Not one of the most popular figures and prices have varied between £125/$225 and £265/$500.

Italian Woman and Italian Man – three pairs have turned up during the past two years and two are still with us but the third was destroyed in transit from the auction room to the buyer. BS: Small crown. SN: Fieldings 20 (the woman), Fieldings 21 (the man). PG: Between £500/$975 and £550/$1100.

Grecian Lady – BS: Small crown. SN: Fieldings 18. Height: 18 inches. PG: £250-£300/$475-$600.

Dancing Girl. BS: Small crown. SN: Fieldings 13. Height 10 inches. PG: £200-£250/$375-$475.

Perhaps there are bargains still to be found. Watch out for. Lady de Bath (Fieldings 19), Peace (Fieldings 22), Lady Sitting (Fieldings 24), Lady Reclining (Fieldings 25), Lady Dancer (large) (Fieldings 26) and Bowl with Lady in Centre (Fieldings 27).

Here is the latest list of Ivrine figures and numbers (1 to 43). Numbers 44 to 56 are brightly coloured high-glaze items of which only a few have been identified.

1	Retriever	29	Girl in semi-nude pose
2	Stork right-hand	30	
3	Stork left-hand	31	
4	Cockerel	32	Lady with Fruit
5	Elephant	33	
6	Newfoundland dog	34	The Bulldog
7	John Bull and dog	35	The Tiger
8	Girl Water carrier	36	The Eagle
9	1914-18 Officer	37	
10	The Fox	38	The Pheasant
11	Madam Pompadour	39	
12	Flower Girl (Red Riding Hood)	40	
13	Dancing Girl (Curtsey)	41	
14	Lady with Jar	42	The Tawny Owl
15	Lady with Jar and Flowers	43	The Hawk
16		44	
17	Gainsborough Girl	45	Miss Muffitt
18	Grecian Lady	46	Sunday Best (Young girl)
19	Lady de Bath	47	Victorian Lady
20	Italian Woman	48	
21	Italian Man	49	
22	Peace	50	
23	Vanity	51	
24	Seated Lady	52	
25	Reclining Lady	53	The Jester
26	Lady Dancer	54	
27	Lady in Bowl	55	
28		56	Parrot on stand

Note. Some of the Ivrine figures were also produced in Bronzine and matt glazed to look like bronze. They are not as popular as the Ivrine figures and this is reflected in the price. At least two Ivrine shapes – Madam Pompadour (11) and Vanity (23) were produced in under-glaze pastel shades. These are very rare.

Dogs . . . dogs . . . and Felix

Man's best friend has always been popular with collectors and Crown Devon dogs are no exception. Prices have climbed steadily over the years which again proves the collectability of Crown Devon products. Many of the champion dog's head studies now top £100/$190. The studies were introduced in the late Thirties by director Neddy Taylor for sale as wall ornaments. There were nine champions in the set modelled by Kathleen Parsons and approved by leading Kennel Club judges. All carry the Thirties backstamp.

Along with Champion Rattlin' Deidre the rest of the champions were:

Modiste of Wolf Glen – Alsatian. SN: 207. Price in 1936 12/6. Price now £120-£140/$220-$275.

Wolstanton Bridgeen – Irish or Airedale terrier. SN: 203. Price in 1936 10/6. Price now £100-£110/$190-$225.

Crackley Supreme Again – Fox terrier. SN: 211. Price in 1936 10/6. Price now £80-£100/$150-$190.

Toydom Man Zee – Pekingese. SN: 202. Price in 1936 7/6. Price now £80-£100/$150-$190.

George of The River – Dalmatian. SN: 214. Price in 1936 12/6. Price now £120-£140/$220-$175.

Heather Realisation – Scottie. SN: 205. Price in 1936 10/6. Price now £90-£110/$175-$225.

Basford Revival – Bulldog. SN: 206. Price in 1936 12/6. Price now £120-£140/$230-$275.

Champion Rattlin' Deidre, a Red Setter.RN: 833379. SN: 222. Price in 1936 10/6. Price now £100-£120.

Exquisite model of Ware, a black, white and tan Cocker Spaniel bitch who won more than 100 trophies.RN: 833375.SN: 204. Price in 1936 10/6. Price now £100-£120.

Part of a Crown Devon pamphlet which was issued by Fieldings in the Thirties. illustrating Art Deco figures by Kathleen Parsons and Sutherland figures, lamps, dogs, and coffee sets etc.

Woeful Willies were made in five sizes between 4 and 10 inches high and in assorted matt glaze colours. The cream and black models which originally cost a few pence more than the others are by far the most popular.

Left: Scottie in high glaze. BS: Thirties in black. SN: 644. Height: 5 inches. PG: £50/$95. Right:. Sealyham in high glaze with collar. BS: Thirties. Height: 7 inches, width 11 inches. PG: £125-£150/$230-$300.

Animals in the doorstop series were: Bulldog, Perky Pup, Scottie, Sealyham, Bunny, Woeful Willie, and Felix. They are quite large figures – Bunny and Scottie are 11 inches high and you may find the sand has been taken out because of the weight of the animals. All are quite rare and prices vary considerably. Perky Pup and Woeful Willie are the most common and fetch between £100/$190 and £135/$275, Scottie, Sealyham and Bunny come in at around £150/$295 and Felix and the Bulldog are top price at £200/$375 plus. As an example of price variation there was a Sealyham at a Malvern antique fair in 1995 at £250/$475 on one stall and £95/$175 on another. The £95/$175 one was snapped up straight away and the £250/$475 one was still there at the end of the day. There is also a small dog – about six inches long – wearing a Bombardier's hat which along with the Churchill bulldog and an 'on to Victory' mug were produced in the early years of the 1939-45 war. If you see a Bombardier dog at under £100/$190, snap him up – he's very collectable. And so is the mug which depicts a soldier, sailor and airman. The price could be £50-£60/$90-$115 or even more.

Three Woeful Willies from the Thirties. BS: Printed or stamped Crown Devon, England, or Fieldings, England. PG: Small £25/$45, medium £50/$95, large with glass eyes £125/235.

Other patriotic items produced at the end of the war were three musical jugs, Rule Britannia, The Star Spangled Banner and There'll Always be an England. These jugs are quite rare and the market value must be in the region of £200-£250/$375-$475.

Talking of war commemoratives, I bid £140/$250 for a Battle of Britain souvenir showing a Spitfire among the clouds and inscribed with Churchill's famous words 'Never was so much owed by so many to so few'. I didn't get it. That was at a London auction about 10 years ago. I have seen only one since at a Midlands fair and that was £275/$525 about five years ago.

It's Felix and friend. BS: Thirties backstamp printed. RN: 811394. Height: 6 inches (probably made in three sizes, the largest about 10 inches). PG: Felix is pretty hard to find and he comes in a variety of colours. The black and white one is the best and fetches around £30/$50 (small), £50-£60/$95-$120 (medium), but the price goes through the roof for the big one – up to and even beyond £200/$375. The dog in the picture is a Thirties model, quite rare, and worth around £30-£45/$50-$80.

A group of Perky Pups. The Perky Pups are probably more popular than the Woeful Willies and the cream and black ones fetch the best prices. BS: Printed or stamped Crown Devon, England. PG: (left to right:). Small green £20/$35, small cream £25/$45, large black and cream with glass eyes £125/$230, small fawn £15/$25.

Doorstop bulldog. This ferocious-looking animal is 11 inches long and 8 inches high and was filled with sand to act as a doorstop. BS: Thirties mark. Decoration. Cream and grey with yellow collar. PG: £200-£250/$375-$500.

Plates and their Prices

Left: The Cottage plate 1950s. BS: Black Crown Devon printed mark. PG: £10-£15/$18-$25. Right: Hunting scene painted by M. Lucas. BS: Large crown circa 1900. PN: Soleilian. PG: £100-£125/$185-$250.

Left: Sèvres plate in ivory ground. 9 inches diameter. BS: Crown on shield. PN: 241. RN: 204438 (1892). PG: £15/$25. Right: Vellum plate - Devon pattern on cream ground. BS: Large crown. RN: 554725. PN: 0734 (1909). PG: £35/$65.

The old and the new. Left: Elm in china. 9 inches diameter. BS: Crown on shield. PN: C215. 1890s. PG: £30-£35/$55-$65. Right: Daffodil plate 9 inches diameter circa 1950s. Printed Crown Devon mark. PG: £10-£15.

Left: Teaplate in Derby pattern 1896. BS: Crown on shield. PN: 453. RN: 287848. PG: £20-£25/$35-$50. Right: Plate in Ryde pattern late 1890s. BS: Crown on shield. PN: 745. PG: £20-£30/$35-$55.

Left: Turin plate in china. BS: Crown on shield. 1890s. PN: C57. PG: £35-£40/$65-$80. Right: Cabinet plate in Royal Essex. BS: Lion on crown. 1890s. PN: 998 (borders in blue, green and fawn). PG: £55-£60/$100-$120.

Left: Fluted plate in Chrysanthemum, sometimes called Royal Windsor. BS: Crown on shield 1890s. PN: 863. PG: £20/$35. Right: Cabinet plate in Elm on cream ground. BS: Crown on shield. PN: X54 1899. PG: £35/$65.

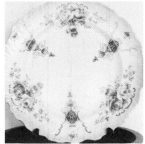

Teck pattern plate. BS: Small crown, Crown Devon, Fieldings. RN: 644307. PN: 0965. PG: £30-£40/$55-$75.

Perth pattern plate. BS: Small crown, Crown Devon, Fieldings. RN: 622805. PN: 0877. PG: £30-£40/$55-$75.

Adams pattern plate. BS: Small crown, Crown Devon, Fieldings. PN: 0781. PG: £30-£35/$55-$70.

Left: Balmoral Castle plate one of six castle plates with dark green border. BS: Large crown early 1900s. PG: £50-£60/$95-$120. Also with light green border. Right: Cranes cabinet plate painted by Marsh. BS: Small crown 1913. PN: 0782 and signed A. Marsh. PG: £200-£250/$375-$500.

Left: Royal Pearl pattern plate. BS: Large crown with lettering 'Royal Pearl copyright'. RN: 519576 1907. PN: 0193. PG: £50-£60/$95-$120. Rare. Right: Handpainted roses cabinet plate. BS: Large crown. PN: 0652 Crown Devon. PG: £100-£120/$195-$230.

Left: Pheasants cabinet plate by Coleman. BS: Small crown 1914. PN: 0865 with signature on painting. PG: £225-£275/$425-$550. Right: Highland cattle plate by G. Cox. BS: Small crown 1913. PN: 0783 with signature on painting. PG: £225-£275/$425-$550. Note: The price margin for these handpainted pieces allows for condition, mint condition plates will certainly fetch top price. A mint condition plate of retrievers painted by R. Hinton may even top £300/$600.

Left: Bird plate on vellum cream ground. BS: Small crown Devon ware. PN: 2026. PG: £35-£45. Rare. Right: Aden pattern plate. BS: Small crown Devon ware. PN: 0232. PG: £35-£45/$65-$90.

Stylised floral pattern wall plaque. BS: Crown Devon stamp post war. Dia 12 inches. PG: £55/$100.

Mavis pattern plate in black with birds and roses design. BS: Small crown, Crown Devon, England. RN: 665351 c1914. PN:1116. PG: £50-£60/$95-$175. A rare piece for a collector but the black patterns are nowhere near as popular as the cream vellum.

Nankin pattern plate. BS: Large crown (early twentieth century). PN: 883. PG: £45-£50/$75-$95.

Plate in Royal Devon Blue pattern. BS: Large crown (early 20th century). PN: X876. PG: £45-£55/$75-$100. Rare.

Salop bread and butter plate. BS: Small crown, Crown Devon, Fieldings. PN: 1169. Diameter 11 inches. PG: £50-£55/$95-$110.

Two top quality Royal Devon plates. BS: Both large crown early 1900s. PN: X543. PG: £50-£60/$95-$120 each.

One of a pair of Royal Clarence vellum plates. BS: Lion on crown with S F and Co above. RN: 206238 - early 1890s. PN: Royal Clarence 996. PG: £100/$195 the pair.

Legends in the Cries of London series were: 'Round and Round, fivepence a pound', 'Old chairs to mend', 'A new love song only a ha'penny apiece' and 'Do you want any matches?'. There were probably others. Watch our for Cries of London plates which were produced in the 1970s, they were darker than the original ones and fetch less than half the price.

There were also Christmas plates produced in the latter years of the company with messages such as 'Along the path of memories sweet at Christmastime old friends will meet' and 'Nearer and closer to our hearts be the Christmas spirit'. PG: £15-£20 / $25-$40.

One of the Cries of London series. BS: Thirties. PN: Round and round, fivepence a pound, Duke cherries. Diameter 10½ inches. PG: £25-£35/$40-$70.

This is a dish from a popular Crown Devon series 'Sailor's Farewell' which was produced during the 1914-18 war. Top of the range was a handsome punch bowl and there were also jugs, mugs, trays and plates. They are quite rare. BS: Small crown, Crown Devon Fieldings. Inscription: 'Sweet, oh Sweet, is that sensation. Where two hearts in union meet: but the pain of separation, Mingles bitter with the sweet'. PG: A plate £25-£30./$45-$55 A dish £15-£20/$25-$35. A mug £20-£30/$35-$55. A punchbowl £100/$190.

Royal Sussex plate in cream vellum. BS: Lion on crown. 1890s. PG: £50-£60/$95-$120.

Crown Devon figures

Fieldings introduced Art Deco figures in the late Twenties and many of them were modelled by Kathleen Parsons. Much of her work was exported all over the world particularly to South Africa, Australia, New Zealand and Canada. These figures along with others by a young Austrian modeller, Olga Hartzeg, are very collectable today – and very expensive, too.

To satisfy home demand in the depression of the Twenties and Thirties, Fieldings introduced the Sutherland figures which were finished in cellulose and so were far cheaper than the glazed variety. Here are a few examples of both cellulose and glazed figures. The PG allows a margin for the Sutherland figures many of which have suffered the ravages of time.

Left: Rio Rita Sutherland figure in cellulose 12 inches high. SN 123. BS: Blue and gold label with the words 'Crown Devon Sutherland figure'. All the Sutherland figures have a decoration number which starts from about F30 and goes up to almost F200. This illustrates the wide range of decoration available to suit customers' requirements. PG: £100-£120/$190-$240. Centre: Rio Rita Sutherland 4 inches high. SN: 168. PN: F171. PG: £50-£60/$95-$120. Right: Rio Rita enamelled and glazed. BS: Crown Devon Thirties mark. SN:123. PN: 2412 with signature K Parsons. PG: £650/$1300 plus.

Left: Priscilla painted and glazed and 6 inches high. BS: CD 30s mark. SN: 130. PG: £150-£175/$275-$340. Centre: Greta the Dutch girl painted and glazed and 6 inches high. BS: CD 30s mark. SN: 143. PG: £150-£175/$280-$350. Right: Lady Anne painted and glazed and 6½ inches high. BS: CD 30s mark. SN: 129. PN: F158. PG: £150-£175/$280-$350. The above figures in cellulose would have a price range between £65/$120 and £85/$150. Cellulose figures in top class condition are tending to rise to £100/$190 and above as they are quite hard to find.

Left: Rare Art Deco figure painted and glazed 13 inches high. BS: CD 30s mark. PN: 2411. PG: £350-£400/$675-$800. Rare. Right: Yvonne by Kathleen Parsons 9½ inches high in matt finish. SN: 155. PN F158. PG: £250/$475. Rare.

Left: Marina in cellulose 7 inches high. BS: Sutherland label. SN: 139. PG: £75-£95/$140-$180. Rare. Right: Juanita in cellulose 7 inches high. SN: 140. BS: Sutherland label. PG: £65-£85/$120-$150.

Left: Sheila in cellulose 5¹/₂ inches high. BS: Sutherland label. SN: 138. Decoration number: F37. PG: £60-£70/$115-$140. Centre: Sonia in cellulose 3¹/₂ inches high. SN: 146. PG: £45-£55/$80-$105. Right: Small Rio Rita in cellulose.

Left: Gloria in cellulose 9 inches high. BS: Sutherland label. SN 137. PG: £60-£75/$115-$140. Right: Priscilla in cellulose 6¹/₂ inches high. SN: 130. PG: £65-£85/$125-$160.

Left: Sutherland figure with mirrors entitled Maytime 12 inches high. BS: Sutherland label. SN: 170. SN of figure Nina 4¹/₂ inches high is 157. PG: £200-£250/$380-$490. Very rare. Note: Only two of these figures have been seen for sale in the last decade. One with a miniature Rio Rita figure was sold a auction in Birmingham in 1992 for close on £100/$190. The figure illustrated was sold at Alexandra Palace in 1993 for £85/$160.

Glazed figure lamp No 6. 12 inches high. Figure: Betty painted and glazed 5¹/₂ inches high and SN 128. PG: £175-£200/$340-$190. With cellulose figure: £125-£150/$240-$300.

Left: Beach Girl by Olga Hartzeg 10 inches high. BS: CD 30s mark occasionally with signature. SN: 226. PG: £450-£500/$875-$1000. Right: Peasant Girl by Olga Hartzeg 10 inches high. BS: CD 30s mark. PG: £400-£450/$775-$900. Rare. Note: A signature on the base of either of these figures could increase the price by a least £50/95. A Peasant Girl was bought by Princess Margaret at a pre-war London exhibition at its original price of 19s 6d/$1.95.

Left: Russian Lady with Borzoi 10 inches high by Olga Hartzeg. BS: CD 30s mark occasionally with signature. SN: 225. PG: £500-£550/$975-$1100. Rare. Beach girl by Olga Hartzeg. BS: CD 30s mark. SN: 226. PG: £500-£550/$975-$1100.

Glazed figure lamp number one, 10¹/₂ inches high. BS: CD 30s mark. Figure: Patricia painted and glazed and SN 136. RN: 799402. PG: £250-£275/$475-$550. With cellulose figure: £150-£175/$295-$350.

Sea Treasures by Kathleen Parsons about 9 inches high. This figure was produced for export in the Thirties and was offered in pastel matt at 10 shillings (50p) or coloured for 11s 6d. BS: CD 30s mark. SN: 185. PG £300/$600 plus.

Another 'treasure' by Kathleen Parsons about 9 inches high. The figure's name and SN is unknown and was produced along with a dozen or so best-sellers which sold extensively in export markets in the Thirties and made Crown Devon a name synonymous with quality across the world. BS: CD 30s mark occasionally with stamp signature. SN: Not known but between 170 and 200. PG £300/$600 plus.

Now, let me introduce you to two figures which I came across on my travels looking for Crown Devon "treasures" a few years ago. It was a pleasure to photograph them (top centre and right) . . . it would be a privilege to own them!

Here for the record are the names and numbers of the daring nude figures by Kathleen Parsons:

171 – Dawn
173 – Grace
175 – Little Butterfly

176 – Sea Breeze
177 – Sea Nymph
178 – Autumn Leaves

Decoration numbers were: Pastel matts: M293 old gold, M294 off white, M295 green and M339 coloured.

Spring by Kathleen Parsons in pastel matt. BS: Sutherland label. Height: 9 inches. SN: 154. PG: £200-£250/$390-$475. (In cellulose £125-£150/$240-$290).

Gina by Kathleen Parsons. BS: Sutherland label. SN: 166. Height: 6¹/₂ inches. PG: £75-£85/$140-$160 in cellulose, £150-£200/$290-$400 glazed.

Caroline by Kathleen Parsons. BS: Sutherland label. SN: 172. Height: 6¹/₂ inches. PG: £75-£90/$140-$180 in cellulose, £150-£200/$295-$400 glazed.

Left: Dancing Waves by Kathleen Parsons. BS: Thirties in gold Crown Devon Fieldings., with small oblong stamp 'By Kathleen Parsons'. SN: 197. Height: 9 inches coloured and glazed. PG: £300/$590 plus. Right: Little Red Riding Hood, wall figure. BS: Thirties. PG: £100-£125/$190-$250.

The English Lady nursery wall figure.

There are six figures in the Nursery Wall series, that are between 6 inches and 8 inches high. They are: The English Lady, The Russian Lady, The Spanish Girl, The Dutch Girl, The Tennis Girl and The Hiker. They carry the CD Thirties mark backstamp. Shape Numbers are: 208, 217, 218, 219, 220 and 221. PG: Prices vary considerably between £100/$190 (the hiker) and £200/$390. Some of the figures are more popular than others but a fair average seems to be around the £150/$295 mark.

When I met Kathleen Parsons several years ago she told me that the Ballerina figure was the best she had ever modelled. I have been looking for her ever since without success but two figures turned up at auction in 1995. One was at Stoke-on-Trent where the figure with some restoration

Old Kate by Kathleen Parsons. BS: Not known. The figure is about 7 inches high. PG: £250/$500 plus. Note: Old Kate sold racecards at Ascot for many many years and sold them to Royalty. King George V was one of her customers. Very rare.

The Ballerina by Kathleen Parsons. BS: Crown Devon Thirties mark with signature by Kathleen Parsons. PN: not known but floral decoration in enamelling and glazed.

Sutherland figure Denise. BS: Label. SN: 158. Height 6½ inches. PG: £75-£85/$140-$160 in cellulose, £150-£200/$290-$375 glazed. Note: Denise comes in two sizes. The small 4 inch model would be considerably cheaper, £45-£65/$85-$120 in cellulose and between £120-150/$220-$290 glazed with Thirties black backstamp.

Glazed figure Sonia. BS: Thirties in black. SN: 146. Height: 3½ inches. PG: £90-£110/$175-$115. In cellulose £45-£55/$85-$110.

fetched a hammer price of around £500/$975. The second was at Rotherham, South Yorkshire, and in perfect condition was knocked down at around the same price. I met the buyer at the Royal Hotel at Ashby de la Zouch where the picture was taken. The owner would not part with the figure for a studio shot and I must admit I don't blame him!!! He valued the figure at £750/$1400.

The Flapper Girl was sold for £1000/$1950 at a London fair about 18 months ago. It is the first Crown Devon figure to touch four figures to my knowledge but it illustrates the increasing value of the Kathleen Parsons pieces. The first Flapper Girl that I saw about four years ago was on offer at £300/$550 and I didn't buy it!

Two other Kathleen Parsons figures which are in the same class are The Bathing Girl and Windy Day which would enhance any collection.

Note: Three pamphlets containing details of a wide range of Sutherland figures and figures by Kathleen Parsons, musical novelties, modern decorative figures, table lamps, dogs' heads also by Kathleen Parsons, and a host of other items are available. (See advert on page ••.)

The Flapper Girl by Kathleen Parsons. BS: Crown Devon Thirties mark with Kathleen Parsons signature. Decoration: Delightful floral pattern enamelled and glazed.

Here's a figure I never expected to see. She's No 137 with decoration F160 and she is in underglaze rather than cellulose but her striking feature is that she is musical. The Swiss movement is housed in a wooden base and plays two waltz tunes. I have seen diagrams of a Sutherland dancing girl but have waited 15 years to see one. She cost £85/$160 and she's not for sale at any price!!!

Royal Worcester? No, Crown Devon

Crown Devon used to be called 'poor man's Worcester'. Not any more, a poor man cannot afford it!!! Signed pieces with paintings of Highland cattle, pheasants, cranes, peacocks and retriever and setter dogs are eagerly sought after – not only by collectors in this country but abroad as well. You can find Royal Worcester practically anywhere, at a price, of course, but Crown Devon pieces are harder to find and that is being reflected in the price. Here are a few examples:

Rose vase by G Cox and two candlesticks. BS: Small crown, Crown Devon, Fieldings. PN: 0681. All signed by G. Cox. SN: 16. Size: 9 inches with cover. Candlesticks 6 inches. PG: Vase £250/$490. Candlesticks £150/$290 the pair.

Pair Cox rose vases 6¹/₂ inches. BS: Small crown, Crown Devon, S F and Co. PN: 0681 both signed G. Cox. SN: 8. Size: 6¹/₂ inches. PG: £250-£275/$490-$550 the pair.

Cranes rose bowl by Marsh circa 1912. BS: Small crown, Crown Devon, England. PN: 0694. Signed A. Marsh. SN: N27. Size: 6 inches. PG: £200-£225/$390-$450.

Pair of pheasant vases by Coleman. BS: Small crown, S F and Co., Crown Devon, England. PN: 0670. Signed J Coleman. SN: 41. Size: 11 inches. PG: £500-£550/$950-$1100.

Left: Miniature dish painted by Hinton. BS: Thirties gold. PN: Dog painting signed by R. Hinton. Diameter: 2¹/₂ inches. SN: Beverley impressed. Legend 'Rationed memories 1917-1947 Neddy'. PG: £100-£120/$190-$240.
Right: Miniature John Peel dish. Here is something more affordable by the average collector. BS: Thirties gold. PN: No number. Signed Walter Lamonby. SN: Beverley impressed. Diameter 2¹/₂ inches. PG: £50-£65/$95-$125. These dishes are sometimes seen in sets of three.

The inscription on the miniature dish by Hinton (bottom left previous page) refers to sales director Ned Taylor who was with the company between 1917 and 1947. Ned, horseman, footballer, tennis player, athlete, cricketer and cyclist was the nephew of Abraham Fielding. Ned died in 1960.

One of a pair of Cox rose vases circa 1912. BS: Small crown S F and Co., Crown Devon. PN: 0681, Devonian. SN: 59. Height: 14 inches. Signed on painting by G. Cox. PG: £500-£600/ $975-$1200.

Cranes urn and cover circa 1911. BS: Large crown, S F and Co., Crown Devon, England. PN: 0694. Signed A. Marsh. SN: 39. Height: 9 inches. PG: £300-£350/$575-$700. Rare.

Nesting Pheasants cylindrical vase circa 1913. BS: Small crown, S F and Co., Crown Devon. PN: 0830. Signed Walter Lamonby. Height: 10 inches. PG: £275-£300/$540-$600.

One of a pair of Fruit vases by F. Harper (1921). BS: Small crown, Crown Devon, Fieldings. PN: 1072. Signed by F. Harper. SN: 96 – 9¹/₂ inches. PG: £600-£650/ $1200-$1300. Note: One of the vases carries its original selling ticket which states '50 shillings the pair'.

One of a pair of Dog vases by Hinton (1914). BS: Small crown, Crown Devon, Fieldings, England. PN: 0929. Signed R Hinton. SN: 43. Height: 9 inches. PG: £550-£600/$1050-$1200 the pair.

Pair of Peacock vases (one restored). BS: Small crown. PN: 0682. One signed W. Stuart, the other H. Stuart. SN: 46 impressed. PG: £225-£275/$430-$550.

Pair of Peacock urns with covers by W. Stuart (1912). BS: Small crown, S F and Co., Crown Devon. PN: 0682. Signed W. Stuart. SN: 14. Height: 7 inches including covers. PG: £300-£350/$575-$750.

Pair of Pheasant vases by Coleman. BS: Small crown S F and Co., Crown Devon. PN: 0670 signed Coleman. Height: 14 inches. PG: £500-£600/$975-$1200.

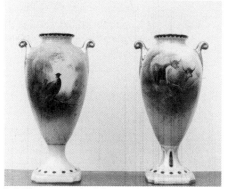

Left: Pheasants vase by Coleman. BS: Small crown, S F and Co., Crown Devon. PN: 0670. Height: 11 inches. PG: £200-£250/$375-$500. Right: Highland Cattle by Cox. BS: Small crown S F and Co., Crown Devon. PN: 0783. SN: 82. Height: 11 inches. PG: £200-£250/$375-$500, more with covers.

Highland Cattle plaque by Cox in oak frame (1913). BS: Small crown, Crown Devon, Fieldings. PN: 0783. Signed on picture G. Cox. PG: £500-£600/$975-$1200.

Plaques were also painted by Walter Lamonby (fruit), R. Hinton (dogs) and J. Coleman (pheasants). They are very collectable and very rare. In mint condition in the original oak frame, the dog plaque would probably lead the field at around £700/$1350 with the rest only ten per cent or so behind. The painted and signed pieces were so successful for a quarter of a century from 1900 onwards that Fieldings introduced a new series when restrictions on decorative ware were relaxed after the 1939-45 war.

They introduced a series of handpainted fancy ware by artists such as Tom Wilcox, N. Carter, S. Dunn and others which were well received in the Fifties and which are attracting Crown Devon collectors today. They are comparatively cheap and could be a good investment for the future. Here are a few examples:

Two nineteenth century Soleilian vases. Left: Horses in Field by M. Lucas circa 1898. BS: Large crown, S F and Co., England. PN: Soleilian. Height: 9 inches. PG: £100-£150/$190-$295. Right: Cattle in River by M. Lucas. BS: Large crown, S F and Co., England. PN: Soleilian. Height: 9 inches. PG: £85-£125/$160-$225. Note: This vase was originally one of a pair. The other vase was signed by Debray.

Two small dishes in Devon Glory (left) and Lady Hamilton series (right). BS: Small Thirties-type mark with Devon Glory and Lady Hamilton script respectively. SN: Left: A 426. Right: A 295. Signed by Carter (left) and Wilcox. PG: Between £40/$75 and £50/$95.

A Roses boat bowl by Wilcox. BS: Thirties-style stamp with 1184 shape number. Decoration: Red and yellow roses painted and signed by Wilcox with delightful matt glazed pink interior finish. PG: £40-£50/$75-$95.

Left: Jug – strawberries by Wilcox. Right: Lady Hamilton roses also by Wilcox. Both are marked Devon Glory and carry a small Thirties-style backstamp. PG: £40-£50/$75-$95 each.

Painters and their patterns (1900-1926)

Dogs

R. Hinton – Small crown backstamp – pattern number 0929.

H. Harris – Large crown backstamp – no pattern number.

Roses

G. Cox – Small crown backstamp – pattern number 0681.

A. Hood – Small crown backstamp – pattern number 0681.

Highland cattle

G. Cox – Small crown backstamp – pattern number 0783.

F. Hancock – Small crown backstamp – pattern number 0790.

Highland Cattle by Cox (1913). BS: Small crown, Crown Devon, Fieldings. PN: 0783. Signed G. Cox. SN: 132. Height: 9 inches. PG: £350-£400/$675-$800 the pair.

Fruit on Porcelain by Lamonby. Size: 15 by 13 inches in oak frame. BS: Small crown, Crown Devon Fieldings. PN: 1072. Signed on picture W. Lamonby. PG: £600/$1200 each or £1250/$2500 for a pair. Very rare.

(Left): Rose vase by Hood. BS: Small crown, Crown Devon, Fieldings. PN: 0681. Height: 11 inches. Signed A. Hood. PG: £300-£350/$575-$700. Note: Ambrose Hood was a Hadley-style flower painter for Royal Worcester in the early twentieth century and left during the 1914-18 war. He did not return to the Worcester factory and this is the only Crown Devon Hood vase the author has seen. Whether he worked at the Devon factory or was a freelance artist is not known.

Left: Front side of rose bowl by Hinton (1914). BS: Small crown, Crown Devon, Stoke-on-Trent. PN: 0929. SN: 6. Height: 6 inches. PG: £300-£350/$575-$700. Right: The other side of the rose bowl by Hinton.

Fruit bowl by F. Cole 12 inches in diameter (1921). BS: Small crown Crown Devon Fieldings. PN: 1072. PG: £200-£250/$395-$500.

Retrievers and pheasants by Lamonby. Size: 21 inches by 9 inches including oak frame. BS: Small crown, Crown Devon, Fieldings. PN: Not known. Signed on picture W Lamonby. Very rare. I have seen a similar painting by R. Hinton. PG: £700-£750/$1350-$1500.

Dog vase by Harris. BS: Large crown (early 20th century). SN: 45. Height: 6 inches. Signed H. Harris. PG: £150-£175/$295-$350. Rare.

Fruit

F. Harper – Small crown backstamp – pattern number 1072.
W. Lamonby – Small crown backstamp – pattern number 1072.
G. Brough – Small crown backstamp – Lustrine fruit.
F. Cole – Small crown backstamp – 1072.

Peacocks

W. Stuart – Small crown backstamp – pattern number 0682.
H. Stuart – Small crown backstamp – pattern number 0682.
Pheasants
J. Coleman – Small crown backstamp – pattern number 0670.
W. Lamonby – Small crown backstamp – pattern number 0830.

Cranes

A. Marsh – Small crown backstamp – pattern number 0694.
J. Lewis -

Stags

G. Cox (pink background) – Small crown backstamp – pattern number 1137.

Highland Cattle by Cox. BS: Small crown, Crown Devon, Fieldings. PN: 0783. Height: 9 inches. Signed G. Cox. PG: £250-£275/$475-$550.

Cattle in Pond
M. Lucas – Large crown backstamp – Soleilian.
Debray – Large crown backstamp – Soleilian.
Horses in Field
M. Lucas – Large crown backstamp – Soleilian.
Debray – Large crown backstamp – Soleilian.
Hunting scene
M. Lucas – Large crown backstamp – Soleilian.
Paintings on porcelain with oak frames
Highland cattle by G. Cox – Small crown backstamp.
Pheasants by J. Coleman – Small crown backstamp.
Dogs by R. Hinton – Small crown backstamp.
Pheasants and Dogs by W. Lamonby – Small crown backstamp.
Fruit by W. Lamonby – Small crown backstamp.
Cranes by A. Marsh – Small crown backstamp.

Rose vase by Cox. BS: Small crown, Crown Devon, S F and Co. PN: 0681. SN: 71. Height: 9½ inches. Signed G. Cox. PG: £250-£300/$475-$600. Rare shape.

This pheasant dish by Coleman sold at an NEC fair in 1995 for £275/$550. That's about the price you would have to pay for a round plaque or plate. They are becoming very hard to find.

Chamber pots and music, too

Fieldings did a brisk trade in chamber pots in the last decade of the 19th century and Sèvres and Indian patterns were very popular in toilet sets which consisted of a jug and bowl, two potties, a slop pail and a soap dish. The vellum series of chamber pots and jugs and bowls etc which followed in the first quarter of the twentieth century were much more decorative and are much more sought after today.

Potties came in all sizes and shapes from miniatures to musicals and vary in price today between a few pounds and £500. Here are a few examples:

One of the nicer 19th century patterns, Suez in white. BS: Crown on shield. PN: 135. PG: £50-£60/$95-$120.

Salop pattern in vellum. BS: Small crown circa 1910. PN: 1129. PG: £50-£60/$95-$120.

Ena pattern in vellum. BS: Small crown circa 1911. RN: 629324. PN: 0999978. PG: £40-£45/$75-$90.

Esk pattern in vellum. BS: Small crown circa 1910. RN: 607505. PN: 0724. PG: £45-£50/$90-$100.

Two miniature potties made in the early days of the 1939-45 war with caricatures of Hitler and Mussolini. Both are two inches in diameter. There are three Hitler miniatures with different words on the side but only one Mussolini. BS: printed Fieldings Made in England. PG: Hitler £35-£45/$65-$90. Mussolini £65-£75/$125-$150.

The potty that's worth a place on any sideboard! BS: Small crown S F and Co., Crown Devon. PN: 0783 signed by G. Cox circa 1912. PG: £200-£250/$380-$500.

Here's the daddy of them all – the white 8¹/₂ inch Hitler musical potty which plays 'Rule Britannia' when lifted. BS: Crown Devon, Fieldings, Made in England. PG: £450-£550/$875-$1100. Very rare.

Perth pattern in white. BS: Small crown circa 1911. RN: 622805. PN: 0876. PG: £30-£35/$55-$70.

Musical chamber pot with a bar scene and the words 'Oh landlord fill the flowing bowl. 8¹/₂ inch diameter. BS: Crown Devon, Fieldings. Inside the bowl there is an eye about 1 inch across in the centre and the words in large letters 'Patent non-splash thunderbowl'. When lifted the potty plays 'Come landlord etc'. PG: £300-£350/$590-$700.
Note: There are two similar potties with different music 'In the Still of the Night' and 'There's a Tavern in the Town'. PG: £300/$600.

Here is the very rare Herman Goering miniature potty depicting the Luftwaffe leader. On the outside it says 'Jerry No.2' and 'Flip your ashes on old piggy'. BS: Printed Fieldings Made in England. PG: around £75. I have heard a rumour that a Dr. Goebbels potty has turned up with a caricature of the propaganda chief. That would be Jerry No.4. Another one which would fetch £75 or more and to think they originally cost no more than a shilling!

Tea and Coffee pots

Coffee pots do not appear to be as collectable as teapots although the Art Deco coffee pots of the Thirties are an exception.

Left: Dora pattern teapot and stand circa 1908. BS: Small crown. RN: 629323. PN: 0871. PG: £100-£120/$190-$235. Right: Royal Stuart teapot and stand circa 1896. BS: Lion on crown. PN: A29. SN: Louis. PG: £125-£140/$240-$275.

Left: Royal Oxford teapot circa 1897. BS: Lion on crown. PN: X94. PG: £100-£110/$190-$220 (with stand). Right: Royal Devon teapot and stand circa 1900. BS: Large crown. SN: Rex. PN: 230. PG: £150/$300 (no stand).

Derby pattern teapot and stand, sugar and cream circa 1896. BS: Crown on shield. PN: 51 and 453. RN: 287848. PG: £100-£125/$190-$250.

'Pewter' pattern teapot, sugar and cream. BS: Small crown with words 'Devon Silverine'. PN: 0690. SN: Hammered. PG: £60-£75/$115-$150.

Unusual shape Royal Devon teapot and stand. BS: Large crown. PN: X543. PG: £150 (allowing for restoration to handle). In perfect condition: £200/$390.

Gold leaf pattern tea kettle circa 1880s. BS: Circular Crown Devon mark. PN: 73. PG: £80-£100/$150-$190.

Teapot, water jug and stand in May in white circa 1914. BS: Small crown. PN: 1186. RN: 689672. PG: £125-£140/$240-$280.

Teapot, stand and water jug in Festoon. BS: Large crown S F and Co. PN: X966 Festoon. SN: Tees. RN: 490296. PG: £150-£200/$290-$400.

Left: Orchid pattern in white circa 1890s. BS: Crown on shield. PN: 27. PG: £50/$95. With stand £75/$140. Right: Elm pattern in brown circa 1900. BS: Large crown. PN: 0236. PG: £30/$55. With stand £55/$100.

Souvenir ware teapot, sugar and cream. BS: Thirties mark. Left to right: St. Ives, Cornwall, parish church Cirencester and Lorna Doone Farm. PG: Teapot £25-£30/$45-$55, cream jug and sugar bowl £15-£25/$25-$45.

Left: Teapot in May. BS: Small crown Crown Devon, Fieldings. PN: 1185. PG: £100-£110/$190-$215. With a stand some £30/$50 more.

Left: Sèvres teapot and stand in white. RN: 204439. PN: 249. SN: Louis. PG: £75-£95/$140-$190. Right: Sèvres tea kettle and stand. BS: Crown on shield S F and Co. RN: 204439. PN: 240. Circa 1892. PG: £75-£100/$140-$200.

Left: Thames teapot and stand circa 1912. Shape: Queen Anne. BS: Small crown. RN: 658031. PN: 1035. PG: £100-£120/$190-$240. Right: Etna teapot and stand circa 1910. Shape: Queen Anne. BS: Small crown. RN: 578617. PN: 0623. PG: £90-£100/$170-$200.

Royal Devon teapot and stand and cream and sugar in plated stand. BS: Large crown circa 1900. PN: X543. PG: Teapot and stand £175-£200/$340-$400. Sugar and cream in stand £125-£150/$240-$290.

Coffee pot in Royal Stuart. BS: Lion on crown S F and Co. PN: A29. SN: Don. Height: 10 inches. PG: £85-£95/$160-$190.

Coffee pot in Royal Clarence. BS: Lion on crown S F and Co. PN: 823. PG: £75-£95/$140-$190.

Coffee pot in Royal Devon. BS: Large crown S F and Co. PN: X712. PG: £90-£110/$175-$220.

Coffee pots. Left: Royal Devon fluted coffee pot circa 1900. BS: Large crown S F and Co. PN: X543. PG: £75-£85/$140-$170. Right: Coffee pot in Orchid circa 1893. BS: Crown on shield. PN: 327. RN: 205280. PG: £60-£70/$115-$140.

A rare Royal Essex teapot. BS: Lion on crown, S F and Co. PN: 998. PG: £100-£125/$190-$250. With a stand it would be worth at least £150/$300.

Silver plated ware

Royal Devon dish. BS: Large crown S F and Co. PN: X712. Diameter 9 inches. PG: £100-£120/$190-$240.

Royal Devon muffin dish. BS: Large crown S F and Co. PN: X482. PG: £60-£80/$115-$160.

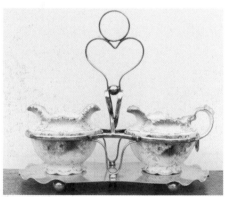

Royal Devon cream and sugar in stand. BS: Large crown S F and Co. PN: X482. PG: £125-£150/$250-$300.

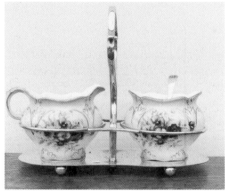

Festoon cream and sugar in stand. BS: Small crown Crown Devon Fieldings. PN: 0713. PG: £100-£125/$200-$250.

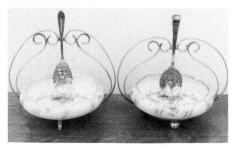

Preserve dishes in plated stands with spoons. BS: Small crown Devon ware Fieldings. PN: 0804 Windsor. PG: £75-£90/$150-$180 each.

Royal Devon dish in stand. BS: Large crown S F and Co. PN: X543. PG: £100-£125/$200-$250.

Three sugar casters. Left: Royal Devon X712 Large crown. Centre: Festoon Royal Devon X963. Large crown. Right: Clyde. No pattern number. Large crown. PG: £35-£50/$65-$95 each.

Sugar and cream in porcelain stand. BS: Large crown S F and Co. RN: 524185. PN: 0373 Crown Devon. PG: £85-£100/$160-$190. Rare.

Bon bon dish in Adams pattern. BS: Small crown, Crown Devon Fieldings. PN: 0781. SN: 120. PG: £50-£65/$95-$130. Rare.

Teapot, sugar and cream in stand. BS: Lion on crown S F and Co. PN: X712. Royal Devon. PG: £150-£200/$300-$400.

This coffee set in a box measuring 25 inches by 21 inches is rather unique. It consists of eight ruby lustrine cups and saucers with enamelled decoration, a plated coffee pot, milk jug, sugar bowl and tongs and eight small spoons. The value? It must be into four figures.

95

Commemoratives

Right: Examples of Crown Devon ware for the Coronation of Queen Elizabeth II in June 1953. Some of the tankards and the cigarette box (A512) had musical movements which played the National Anthem. BS: Thirtes mark. The illustration proves that this mark was carried on into the Fifties. PN: As illustrated. PG: Well worth collecting before they get too expensive although some of the pieces especially those with musical movements are already over the £100/$200 mark.

A rare Boer War commemorative jug. BS: Lion on crown. PN: X184 and named Royal Khaki. SN: Bute. PG: £100-£120/$190-$250.

Commemoratives galore: This fine collection of Crown Devon commemorative ware was sent in by a lady in Cumbria. It shows a variety of mugs and beakers in both ivory and cream vellum and produced to mark the coronation of King George V and Queen Mary on June 22nd 1911. The majority have a registration number of 563731 and all carry the large crown backstamp. The pattern number on the jug at the back is 0578. Some of the pieces carry the same number but others have pattern No. 0584. PG: This isn't an easy one. Devon commemoratives are not easy to find and they have increased in price dramatically this last few years. I have known ivory mugs and beakers as low as £20/$35 – and cream vellum mugs as much as £70/$150.

1911 Coronation cup and tankard. BS: Large crown with the words 'Devonware S F and Co., Stoke-on-Trent, England'. PN: 0578. PG: In white £35-£45/$65-$90 each. In vellum £55-£75/$100-$150 each.

Three heroes of yesteryear

Three more commemorative beakers have come to light in the last few months of 1996 to add to the one produced by Fieldings in memory of Edward the Peacemaker. Off-white with a black rim, this beaker has the King's picture on the front with the words 'King and Emperor'. On the base is the large crown S F & Co. It is worth between £70/$140 and £80/$160.

The three 'finds' are all similar beakers but have a gold rim instead of a black one. They are about four inches high and all carry the crown on shield backstamp. They are:

This is the Peace mug produced by Fieldings after the First World War. Marked Devon ware S F and Co, the front depicts Britannia and the flags of allied nations. PG: £50-£60/$95-$120.

Lieutenant Colonel R. S. S. Baden Powell
General Sir Redvers Buller VC
General Lord Kitchener of Khartoum

They appear to have been made at the same time as two, Kitchener and Buller, have the same pattern number, X189. They all have pictures on the front (General Buller is in blue) and they have different wording, of course. They are very rare. If you find them, expect to pay £100/$200 for each beaker.

Holiday memories . . .

Crown Devon launched the souvenir ware series in the early Thirties to cater for the holiday trade as millions of people bought mementoes of their week by the sea or in the country. There were little cream jugs in different sizes and shapes with the legend 'Happy memories of Rhyl' and so on.

There were little dishes, coffee cans and cups and saucers. There was the small teapot and the miniature cheese dish but it's the cream jugs that have caught the collector's eye and prices of these have increased 200 per cent or more during the past few years.

Crown Devon also received orders for these souvenir novelties from South Africa and America and examples of these items are very collectable. One was done for Lincoln's home in Illinios.

Far left: A salt cellar with the inscription 'Lincoln's Home', Springfield, Illinois. Near left: The Crown Devon backstamp with the words 'Made in Staffordshire, England, and imported for the Lincoln Centre, Springfield, Illinois'. PG: £20-£25/$35-$45.

Here are other examples of souvenir ware with printed pictures of places of interest throughout the UK (all carry the Thirties backstamp).

Three little cream jugs. Left: Lincoln Cathedral. Centre Cockington Forge. Right: Colwyn Bay. PG: £10-£15/$18-$25. Occasionally to be found cheaper.

Three little jugs in different shapes. Left to right: Arundel Castle; Quayside, Cornwall; Pump Room, Harrogate. PG: £8-£12/$15-$25.

Two souvenirs of North Yorkshire. Left: Sauce boat with legend 'Happy memories of Richmond'. Right: Mug with 'Happy memories of Ripon'. PG: £12-£15/$25-$30.

Two pieces from Bonnie Scotland. Left: Cream Jug from Kinross. Right: 'Royal Stuart' from the Tartan series. PG: £12-£15/$25-$30.

Here for the record are more of the places so far identified in the souvenir series:
North Front, Blenheim Palace.
Widdicombe, Dartmoor.
Lindisfarne Priory, Holy Island.
Lulworth Cove.
Balmoral Castle.
The Esplanade, Minehead.
Salisbury Cathedral.
East Cliff, Folkestone.
Bath Abbey.
Windsor Castle.
Cockington Forge, Torquay.
Hexham Abbey.
The Malvern Hills.
Jersey.
Guernsey.
Cheddar.
Bourton on the Water.
The Pump Room, Harrogate.
Happy memories of Knaresborough.
Glastonbury Abbey.
The Ship Inn, Porlock.
Thoresby Hall.
Weymouth Harbour.
St. Ives, Cornwall.
Castle Gardens, Dunoon.
Hunters Inn, Exmoor.
Happy Memories of Morecambe.
Colwyn Bay.
Lucky Cornish Pixies, St. Ives.
Flora McDonald's Statue, Inverness.
Kinross.
Castle Gateway, Skipton.
Loch Lomond and Ben Lomond.
Abbey Sands, Torquay.
Arundel Castle.
The three reaches of Ullswater.
Windsor Castle from the Thames.
Kingussie.
The Esplanade, Weymouth.
Valley of the Rocks, Linton.
Quayside, Cornwall.
Cross Castle, Inverary.
Symonds Yat, Wye Valley.
Llangollen Bridge.
Lincoln Cathedral.
The Island, Newquay.
The Esplanade, Troon.
The Bay, Douglas, Isle of Man.
The Green, Silloth.

A dish 10 by 6 inches showing Cross Castle, Inverary. In front: Preserve jar Walton-on-the-Naze, salt cellar Robin Hood and Major Oak and small jug 'n bottle Royal Pavilion, Brighton. PG: Dish £15-£20/$25-$35. The rest: £10-£15/$19-$30 each.

Left to right: Sugar dish The Esplanade, Minehead, teapot Paighton, and coffee can The Esplanade, Minehead. PG: Dish £15/$25, teapot £20-£25/$35-$45 and coffee can £15-£20/$25-$35. The coffee can with a saucer would cost another £5/$10.

Left: cup and tray set showing Weymouth Harbour. Right: Cheese dish showing John O'Groats. PG: £20-£25/$35-$45 each.

Richmond, North Yorkshire.
Blacksmith's shop, Gretna Green.
Kendal Nether Bridge.
Walter Scott's Monument.
Derwent Water from Ashness Bridge.
Old Bridge of Dee.
My Lady of the Lake on Ullswater.
Happy Memories of Ripon.
Luss village, Loch Lomond.

John O'Groats overlooking Stroma.
Seaside, Combe Martin.
The Harbour, Looe.
York Minster, West Front.
Bakewell Bridge, Derbyshire.
The Norfolk Broads.
Knaresborough from Castle Hill.
The Monastery, Fort Augustus.
The Parade, Walton-on-the-Naze.
Robin Hood and the Major Oak.
Polperro, Cornwall.
Portmadoc Harbour.
Westminster Abbey.
Royal Stuart.

The Royal Pavilion, Brighton.
Old Houses, Taunton.
Barmouth Viaduct and Cader Idris.
Huntley Castle.
The Tower, Christ Church, Oxford.
Fragrant memories of Penmaenmawr.
A souvenir of Widdicombe.
Gloucester Cathedral.
And there will be many more.

The two from abroad:
South Africa – Mostert's Mill.
America – Lincoln's Home, Springfield, Illinois.

Believe it or not, both these sets of graduated jugs are Royal Devon. The top three are Riga Royal Devon, pattern number X877, large blue crown and gilding on royal blue ground. Below: three jugs with pattern number X543, large crown with flowers on cream ground. PG Both sets worth around £250/$500.

Into the Fifties

Crown Devon produced an interesting range of stylised contemporary wares during the 1950s. These relied on the use of the curved line to achieve their effect, a stark contrast to and reaction against the angular and geometric shapes of pre-war years. Three of the patterns which have become very collectable are Stockholm, Greenland and Pegasus. Here are a few examples:

Three examples of Stockholm fancy ware illustrating the factory's skill in design and decoration. BS: Crown Devon, Fieldings. PG: £35-£45/$65-$85 each piece.

Stockholm coffee pot and cup and saucer, part of a set. BS: Crown Devon, Fieldings. PG: £60-£80/$115-$160 the set.

A fine collection of Stockholm ware. BS: Crown Devon, Fieldings. PG: A tea service c£150/$300. A dinner service £200/$400.

Table ware in Stockholm (red) and Greenland (green). BS: Crown Devon, Fieldings. PG: Cup and saucer £10/$18. Teaplate £5/$10. Milk jug £10/$18. Salt cellar £10/$18.

Pegasus in gold.This striking Pegasus design cup is flanked by two decorative jugs. BS: Fifties Crown Devon stamp. PG: Cup: £15-£25/$30-$50. Jugs: £15-£20/$30-$40.

Two small jugs and gilded ornament. BS: Fifties Crown Devon. PG: £10/$18 each.

101

Pegasus vase in black. BS: Crown Devon, Fieldings. Height: 5 inches. PG: £25-£35/$45-$70. Note. Pegasus was named by Mary Fielding, widow of Reginald Fielding, the last managing director of the company. The most popular colour was red but the top quality wares were in black with white and brown horses and decorated in gold. A 10 inch top quality vase was seen at Newark in 1993 at £125/$250.

Part of a collection of Stockholm by a lady in Norwich who started collecting for her bottom drawer in the early Fifties and hasn't stopped since. PG: You can't put a price on a collection of memories!

Left: Chelsea Pensioner. Right: Scottie. PG: £55-£60/$100-$120 each.

Attractive gold ornament.BS: 1950s or later in gold with small crown. SN: 1486. Height: 6 inches. PG: £10/$18.

Teapot, sugar and cream in gold. BS: Fifties mark. PG: £45/$90 the set.

Coaching Days series: Manor House, Oxford. Sugar and milk set and dish. BS: Fifties Crown Devon. PG: Dish £15/$25, the set £20-£30/$35-$60. Note. The Coaching Days plates which have pictures of different coaching day halts are quite collectable and are priced at around £25/$50.

Left: Dick Turpin. Right: Novelty teapot. PG: £45-£55/$85-$110 each.

The late Fifties saw the introduction of a series of biscuit jars which are becoming increasingly popular in kitchens of the 1990s. They are Perky Pup (No. 1045), Humpty Dumpty (No. 1049), The Clown (No. 1050), The Teddy Bear (No. 1051), Peter Pieman (No. 1061) and Scottie (No. 1062).

These are all between 10 inches and 13 inches tall and today are worth between £40/$80 and £50/$100 each. But like so much of the Fifties, Sixties and Seventies products, they can be found much cheaper. I heard recently of a Welsh collector who strolled into an auction and bought Peter Pieman and six other novelty pieces for £14/$30. That made his day!

Here's someone to cheer you up on a Monday morning when the housework is getting on your nerves. It's The Clown, No.1050, one of a series of biscuit jars. Ideal for the kitchen and not too expensive at around £50-£60/$95-$120.

The Squirrel. BS: Fifties stamp. PG: £70-£90/$130-$180.

This photo showing two large jugs from the Cries of London series came from New Zealand, courtesy Jill and Roger Hill, of Tauranga. They, and many others tehre, are avid collectors of musicals and other Crown Devon ware. I believe prices there are cheaper, too.

Jugs in all shapes and sizes

Here is a selection of jugs in all shapes and sizes from the late 19th century to the Thirties:

Jug in Wells, bowl in Elm blue. Jug BS: Large crown. PN: 662. SN: Tweed. Height: 11 inches. PG: £50-£60/$95-$120. Bowl BS: Crown on shield. PN: X73 Elm with blue border. PG: £40-£50/$75-$95.

Water jug and cream jug in Silverine. BS: Large crown Devon ware circa 1900. PN: 0690 Silverine. PG: £15-£20/$25-$50. With teapot and sugar basin £55-£65/$100-$130.

Three graduated jugs in Etna. BS: Small crown circa 1910. RN: 578617. SN: Queen Anne. PG: £140-£160/$260-$350.

Three Pearline graduated jugs. BS: Large crown circa 1900. Sizes: 7 inches, 7½ inches and 9 inches. PG: £100-£120/$190-$250.

Large jug in Clyde. BS: Large crown S F and Co., England. PN: X248 Clyde. PG: £50-£60/$90-$120.

Exotic birds jug. BS: Large crown S F and Co. PN: 0325 Crown Devon. RN: 334424. SN: Impressed Albion. PG: £100-£120/$190-$240.

Grecian jug in blue. BS: Large crown in blue. S F and Co. PN: 0156. SN: Peel. Height: 13 inches. PG: £70-£80/$140-$160.

Jug and bowl in Esk. BS: Small crown, Crown Devon. RN: 617593 circa 1910. PN: 0724. SN: Wells. PG: £200-£250/$390-$500.

Jug and bowl in Pendant. BS: Large crown Devon ware. PN: 0474. SN: Iona. RN: 555509. PG: £200-£250/$390-$500.

Jug and bowl in Spring. BS: Small crown, Crown Devon. PN: 1000. PG: £250-£300/$470-$600.

Jug and bowl in white. BS: Large crown. PN: Oban. PG: £150-£200/$290-$400.

Small jug and pepper pot. BS: Large crown S F and Co., Crown Devon. RN: 554725. PN: 0465. Height: 4 inches. Pepper pot 3 inches. PG: £20-£30/$35-$60. Pepper pot £10-£15/$18-$25.

Three graduated jugs in Indian. BS: Ribbon mark circa 1890s. PN: 625. PG: £120-£140/$230-$280.

Small jug in Royal Lorne. BS: Lion on crown S F and Co. PN: A24. Height: 4½ inches. PG: £30-£35/$55-$70.

Jug in Perth in white. BS: Small crown Devon ware Fieldings. PN: 0870. SN: Ritz. RN: 622805. PG: £60-£65/$115-$130.

Art Deco jug. BS: Thirties in blue. PN: Mattita. Height: 7½ inches. PG: £120-£150/$230-$300.

Slop pail circa 1898. BS: Large crown S F and Co. PN: 018 Royal Devon. This pattern was later called Ribbon. Height: 11½ inches. PG: £100-£120/$190-$240.

Dressing table set in Teck. BS: Small crown, Crown Devon Fieldings. RN: 644367. PN: 0965 Teck. PG: Hat pin holder £35/$70. Soap dish £30/$60. Heart-shaped dish £40/$80. Tray £40/$80. Three small dishes £30-£40/$60-$80. Candlesticks (not shown) £40-£50/$80-$100. Total for set £200/$400.

Pearline coffee jug and cream and sugar. BS: Large crown on coffee pot. Crown on shield on cream and sugar circa 1898. PN: X194. PG: £80-£100/$150-$190.

Royal Devon jugs circa 1890. BS: Circular stamp. Royal Devon. SN: 334. No pattern number and unusual floral design. PG: £75-£95/$150-$200.

Jardinières

Here are a few jardinières which are very popular with Crown Devon collectors:

Two plant holders. Left: Nankin. BS: Large crown. S F and Co. PN: X883 Nankin. 1905. Right: Crown on shield. S F and Co. PN: 957. Crown Chelsea. Late 1890s. PG: £60-£80/$115-$160 each.

Jardinière in Pendant in cream vellum. BS: Large crown S F and Co. RN: 555509. PN: 0472. SN: York 9 inches. PG: £110-£130/$210-$275.

Royal Devon jardinière. BS: Circular mark circa 1886. PN: Royal Devon. PG: £75-£85/$140-$175.

Jardinière in Pendant in ivory. BS: Large crown, Devon ware. RN: 555509. PN: 0469. SN: Ebor 9 inches. PG: £75-£95/$140-$200.

Royal Tudor jardinière. BS: Lion on crown late 1890s. SN: Oban 9 inches. PN: X62. PG: £80-£100/$150-$190.

Jardinière in Thames in white. BS: Crown on shield circa 1896. PN: 167 Thames. SN: Thistle. PG: £50-£60/$95-$120.

Jardinière in Salop pattern. BS: Small crown, Crown Devon, Fieldings. PN: 1169. Height: 8 inches, diameter 8½ inches. PG: £100-£120/$190-$240.

Jardinière in Erin pattern. BS: Small crown Crown Devon S F and Co. RN: 611251. Height: 6 inches. PN: 0737. PG: £100-£120/$190-$250.

Royal Devon jardinière. BS: Large crown S F and Co. PN: X543 PG: Jardinière £600/$1200, with stand £1000-£1250. Note. This jardinière carries an inscription: Souvenir of 21 years continuous service with S Fielding and Co., Ltd., Stoke-on-Trent. It is one of 19 jardinières and stands presented to employees by Abraham Fielding in 1911. One has been bought by a Japanese visitor and taken home to Tokyo.

Royal Devon jardinière and collar. BS: Large crown. S F and Co. PN: X543. 1902. Height: with collar 19 inches, diameter (including handles 17 inches), height with stand 42 inches. PG: With collar and stand £1250-£1500/$2500-$3000.

Two mugs in Erin. BS: Small crown Crown Devon S F and Co. RN: 611251. PN: 0737. PG: £120-£140/$240-$280 the pair.

Jardinière and stand in Pearline. BS: Large crown Devon ware circa 1900. PN: X194. Height: 11 inches. PG: £70-£90/$135-$190.

Jardinière stand in Festoon Royal Devon 1899. BS: Large crown. S F and Co. Also impressed Fieldings. PN: X96. Height: 23 inches. PG: £250-£300/$500-$600.

Two miniature jardinières. Both late 1890s. Far left: Royal Oxford. Lion on crown S F and Co. PN: 94. Height: 4½ inches. Near left: Royal Tudor. BS: Lion on crown. PN: X62. Height: 4 inches. PG: £70-£80/$140-$160.

Three-handled mug. BS: Large crown S F and Co. RN: 414507. PN: 0313 Crown Devon. PG: £75-£95/$140-$200. Rare.

Two-handled mug in Teck. BS: Small crown Crown Devon Fieldings. RN: 644307. PN: 0965. PG: £75-£85/$150-$175.

Rose and fruit bowls

Rose and fruit bowls come in various shapes and sizes and prices vary between £50/$95 and £150/$300 for pieces in good condition. Here are a few examples:

Fruit bowl in Wick. BS: Small crown Crown Devon. RN: 648631. PN: 0992 Wick 1915. PG: £90-£110/$175-$220.

Rose bowl in Perth. BS: Small crown, Crown Devon. RN: 622805. PN: 0853. Perth 1913. PG: £110-£130/$220-$275.

Rose bowl early 1900s. BS: Large crown Devon ware, S F and Co. PN: 0192. SN: 67. PG: £40-£50/$75-$95.

Royal Devon fruit bowl. BS: Large crown S F and Co. PN: X543. Diameter 8 inches. PG: £100-£120/$95-$250.

Two-handled bowl in Aden. BS: Large crown S F and Co. PN: X997. 1906. PG: £100-£120/$190/$240.

This superb Royal Devon bowl with large gilt handles is most unusual. BS: Large crown early 1900s. PN: X543. PG: £120-£150/$240-$300 (could be more). This is one for the connoisseur.

Perth bowl with handles. BS: Small crown, Crown Devon, Fieldings. RN: 622803. PN: 0853. PG: £70-£85/$140-$175.

10 inch diameter bowl in Erin. BS: Small crown, Crown Devon, Fieldings. PN: 0737. 1912. PG: £65-£85/$130-$170.

Fluted dish in Etna. BS: Small crown, Crown Devon S F and Co. RN: 578617. Diameter: 9 inches. SN: 257. PG: £60-£70/$115-$150.

Baby plate in Royal Devon. BS: Large crown S F and Co. PN: X712 Crown Devon. PG: £50-£70/$190-$140. Rare.

Rose bowl in Wick. BS: Small crown, Crown Devon Fieldings. RN: 648631. PN: 0992. PG: £140-£160/$275-$325.

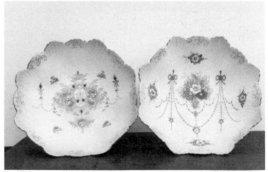

Fruit comports in Wick and Banff. Left: Wick pattern. BS: Small crown (1915). RN: 648631. PN: 0992. SN: Bath 10 inches. PG: £85-£100/$160-$200. Right: Banff pattern. BS: Small crown (1910). RN: 577373. PN: 0598. SN: Bath 10 inches. PG: £85-£100/$160-$200.

They take the biscuit

Biscuit barrels (all about 6 inches high).

Left: Royal Oxford circa 1900. BS: Lion on crown. SN: 11. PN: X164. PG: £75/$140. Right: Royal Lorne late 1890s. BS: Lion on crown. PN: A24 PG: £75/$150

Left: Daisy pattern circa 1912. BS: Small crown. PN: Devon ware Daisy. SN: 42. PG: £70-£80/$135-$175. Right: Royal Kew late 1890s. BS: Lion on crown. PN: A33. PG: £65/$135.

Royal Sussex barrel late 1890s. BS: Lion on crown. PN: A18. Height: 8½ inches. PG: £100-£120/$195-$250.

Early Royal Devon barrel. BS: Lion on crown. PN: X872 Royal Devon. SN: 42. PG: £70-£90/$140-$190.

Unusual three-handled biscuit barrel. BS: Lion on crown. SN: 37. PN: Royal Devon X712 (green and orange design). PG: £80-£100/$150-$200. Rare.

Left: Exotic birds barrel. BS: Lion on crown. PN: 0325. SN: 49. PG: £75-£85/$150-$175. Rare. Right: Exotic birds ewer circa 1900. BS: Large crown. PN: 0325. SN: Albion. Height: 15 inches. PG: £100-£140/$190-$275. Rare.

John Peel biscuit barrel. BS: Thirties. Crown Devon printed. PG: £80-£90/$150-$190. Rare.

Left: Crown Chelsea plant holder. BS: Crown on shield. PN: 857. Height: 5½ inches. PG: £50-£60/$95-$120. Right: Crown Chelsea circa 1890s. BS: Crown on shield. PN: 857. PG: £60-£75/$120-$175.

Clyde dish 10½ inches by 8½ inches. BS: Large crown. PN: X248 circa 1900. PG: £40-£50/$75-$100.

Saxon dish 11 inches by 9½ inches. BS: Large crown. PN: X722. 1904. PG: £75-£85/$150-$175.

Peek Frean biscuit barrel. This piece carries no identification marks but is believed to have been one of two biscuit barrels made for Peek Frean. PG: £40-£50/$75-$95.

Royal Clarence dish 11 by 8 inches. BS: Lion on crown late 1890s. PN: 23. PG: £35-£45/$70-$90.

112

Golfing memorabilia

This Thirties golfer ashtray in Mattita ware was seen at an auction with a golfing condiment set pictured below. Both had the Thirties stamp and the condiment set was a golfing figure on a green base with the word 'Fore'. The three golf balls were salt, pepper and mustard. The hammer price for the pair was over £200/$400. Another gem to look for in the series is a footballer about three inches high in Stoke City colours (red and white stripes).

Here is Fieldings 47 from the Ivrine range – she arrived just too late to be included in the Ivrine section. Her white dress is trimmed with green and she has a large pale blue hat. BS: Small crown Crown Devon Ivrine and impressed Fieldings 47. PG: £250-£300/$500-$600.

Striking clocks

The best clocks by Simon Fielding and Co were made between 1896 and 1901 with movements by the British United Clock Company whose name is engraved on the backplate. They were mostly 8-day clocks and struck on the hour and the half-hour. Bedroom clocks with a 30-hour movement were made in the years just before and just after the turn of the century but very few of these movements have survived. Here are a few examples of Fieldings clocks which are both very rare and very expensive:

Left: Blue and white clock with original 30-hour movement circa 1898. BS: Crown on shield. Height: 8½ inches. PG: £300-£350/$600-$700. Right: Bedroom clock in white in Fife pattern circa 1898. BS: Crown on shield. PN: 04. Height: 8 inches. PG: £125-£150/$250-$300.

Vellum clock in Crown Devon pattern with new German 30-hour movement. BS: Large crown circa 1909. RN: 554725. PN: 0465. Height: 11½ inches. PG: £200-£250/$400-$500.

This eight-day clock carries a crown on shield backstamp and has a Japy Frere movement. The pattern is 'Rustic'. The owner says "It's a real gem and very expensive".

Collectors' Corner

Here are a few items that you won't find every day but they help to make Crown Devon collecting such an enjoyable – and at times – rewarding hobby. They vary in price from a few pounds to a few hundred. Most of these pictures were sent in by collectors which accounts for the variable quality of the photos.

A cruet set from the Fieldings stable. It bears the post war stamp. Value unknown.

The Berry Inn, one of the Old Inn series. BS: Thirties in blue. PN: Mattita. Height: 4 inches. PG: £45-£50/$90-$100.

The Cockerel and Duckling cruet set. BS: Thirties black stamp. PG: £40-£45/$80-$90.

The Pixie jam pot. BS: Thirties mark but these items were produced into the Fifties. SN: 622. PG: £30-£40/$50-$80.

Miniature plant pot in Shield pattern. BS: Small crown, Devon ware. Height: 4 inches. PN: 1090. RN: 662837. SN: Beaded. PG: £40-£50/$75-$100.

The Cockerel and Family vase. BS: Large crown early 1900s. PN: X477 with words 'Trentham art ware'. SN: 49. Height: 9 inches. This vase, handpainted and signed C. Hindley, is the only one I have seen in 15 years. It is an example of Ye Olde English ware. PG: It cost £85/$175, but could be worth much more to a keen collector.

Royal Devon china tea service. BS: Large crown early 1900s. PN: X543. PG: You won't find many of these about, either. If you do, expect to pay well over £1000/$1900. Royal Devon china trios are fetching more than £100/$190.

The Guardsman. One of a wide range of character jugs produced in the Sixties by Shorter and Sons following the takeover by Fieldings. The size and model name is impressed on the base and some carry the Shorter mark and some Crown Devon. The models include: Beefeater, Cavalier, Dick Turpin, Guardsman, Hayseed, Long John Silver, Neptune, Pensioner, Scottie, Sheik and Pedro. PG: Prices vary a great deal but the average appears to be £40-£55/$75-$110.

Plaque by Hinton. Here is a 9½ inch plaque with a painting by R. Hinton of retrievers. Signed on the picture and with a wide gold border, the plaque carries the small crown backstamp. The photo was sent in by a collector from Scunthorpe. His valuation: £350/$700. Note: The handpainted plaques were half an inch wider than handpainted plates and are favoured by most collectors. I'd settle for either!!!

Pint mug for a Tyke. This pint mug carries the Thirties backstamp but was probably made in a novelty series both before and after the '39-45 war. It carries the Yorkshireman's anthem 'See all, hear all, say nowt. Eat all, drink all, pay nowt. And if ever tha does out for nowt, do it for thissen'. PG: For a Yorkshireman £20/$35 or more. For a Lancastrian: He wouldn't have it given.

Cruet set in Wye pattern. Quite a rare set with a registration number of 635583 and a pattern number of 0560. Introduced around 1914 and very collectable. PG: £65-£85/$125-$175.

Little Pigs baby plate. BS: Large crown (early 1900s) and probably one of a series of farm animals. PG: It cost £2/$4 at an outside stall at Peterborough. Would you pay more!!!

Gift for the gentleman? This unusual piece with the Elm pattern decoration and carrying a large crown backstamp was produced at the turn of the century. It is 5 inches high and has a tight-fitting silver-plated cover. What is it? One suggestion is that it is a gent's Cologne bottle. It was bought for £28/$55 at a Buxton pavilion gardens fair in 1989. It's value today? About £40/$75.

Commemorative tobacco jar. This handsome piece commemorating the coronation of King George V and Queen Mary was found in Bermuda in 1991. The cost £100/$190. It would fetch nearly double that at auction in the UK today.

Royal York coffee pot. Rare floral design on a Royal York coffee pot of the last century. Contributed by Don of Chester. BS: Lion on crown. RN: 203239. PG: £50-£70/$95-$150.

Victorian elegance. Two large jardinières and stands, the one on the left in Royal Devon pattern (X543) and the other in Crown Devon pattern (RN 554725). PG: Royal Devon £1250/ $2500, Crown Devon £1000/$2000.

Left: The Quince honey pot. BS: Printed stamp 'Quince Aviaries, South Molton, Devon, Made by Fieldings, Devon Pottery'. SN: 509. PG: £30-£35/$55-$75.

Right: Royal Devon three-handled loving cup. BS: Large crown. PN: X543. PG: £100/$190.

Royal Devon dessert service. There are six plates, two comports and two dishes. BS: Large crown. PN: X543. PG: Between £500-£600/$975-$1200.

Alton Towers plaque. Here is the third plaque in the series. Haddon Hall and Trentham Hall are the other two. PG: £500-£550/$975-$1100.

Inkwell in Thames pattern. BS: Small crown. RN: 658051. PN: 1025. PG: £80-£100/$150-$200. Very rare. Nice one, Marie.

Royal Devon cheese dish. BS: Large crown. PN: X543. SN: Rex 10 by 7 inches. PG: £150-£170/$300-$350.

The Cheddar Cheese. One of the 'Old Inn' range of cheese dishes, biscuit barrels and jam pots. This cheese dish is quite rare as are 'The Berry Inn', the jampot, and 'The Baker's Inn', the biscuit barrel. BS: Thirties printed stamp in black. PN: 664. PG: £50-£60/$90-$120. The Berry Inn would be between £40-£50/$75-$95 and the Baker's Inn just a little more.

An ashtray with a painting by Tom Wilcox of Simon of Trentham.

A child's nursery musical mug. One of a series of nursery novelties produced in the Thirties, this Little Red Riding Hood mug is quite rare. It plays 'Who's Afraid of the Big Bad Wolf?' PG: £45-£55/$90-$110.

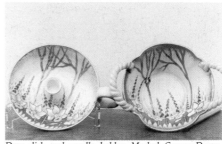

Deco dish and candle holder. Marked Crown Devon, Fieldings, and carrying the Thirties mark, here are two pieces of 'Springtime' with pattern number M460. PG: £50-£55/$95-$110 each.

No collection is really complete without Felix the cat who comes in various colours and sizes. He can be bought for between £45/$90 and £100/$200 depending on size, the top model being black and white and about nine inches tall. The blue Felix here is worth about £50-£60/$100-$120 and his doggy friend about £30-£35/$55-$75.

An Easter egg? This small pot egg with the Devon Ware stamp and a pattern number of 0505 was introduced around 1911 with a forget-me-not decoration and is believed to have been given to ladies as a keepsake. There were many different designs. PG: £30-£35/$55-$75.

Tea for two. BS Small crown, Crown Devon, Fieldings. PN: Etna 0623 1916. PG: £100-£120/$190-$250 with one cup missing. £150/$300 if complete.

1950s coffee set. Springwood is the name of this attractive coffee pot and cup and saucer from a set of six. With milk jug and sugar basin it is valued at around £85/$175.

A novelty egg cup set with cockerel handle produced in the Fifties and Sixties. Sold for a few shillings. Now worth a few pounds.

Coleman coffee set. There are two coffee cans and saucers missing but this lovely set signed on each piece by artist J. Coleman was produced just before the First World War. It is valued at between £500/$1000 and £600/$1200 by the collector who sent in the photo.

Bathing Girl. This Thirties figure 'Bathing Girl' appears in the Crown Devon booklet published in the Thirties entitled 'Figures and lamps and gift suggestions'. Under the heading "Modern decorative figures" she is one of six figures, is 10¹/₂ inches high and No. 124. The price then: 19s 6d. The price now: £600-£650/$1150-$1300. She belongs to a lady in Cardiff. The other figures are: No. 60 Beach Girl, No. 62 Kiki, No. 121 Windy Day, No. 125 Yachting Twins and No. 127 Rosemary. The Bathing Girl is probably the most expensive but the Yachting Twins won't be far behind.

Here's Dawn, a favourite figure in the Thirties from the Kathleen Parsons selection. Numbered 171 she was often the attraction in Art Deco lamps which sold for just over £1/$2. The lamps are not often seen today but the figures are still around in off white, green and old gold. These figures start at £250/$500 but others such as Dancing Waves and Sea Treasures go beyond the £300/$600 mark. I saw Summertime at Stratford Antiques Centre some 18 months ago and she was on her way to the USA for around $450/$900.

Windy Day is No. 121 in the 'Modern decorative figures' produced at the Devon Pottery in the Thirties. She was also made as a cellulose figure but is far more attractive in underglaze in her pale pink dress and black shoes with her auburn hair flowing in the breeze. I value her at around £300-£350/$700 but her owner would probably add £100/$200 to that!

Here's Carnival, No.156 in the Sutherland series shown in the Thirties brochure. 9" high, the figure in the book is cellulose and painted in decoration No. F154. I'd value that one at close on £200/$400 but this one goes a step further. It's underglaze, it's out of this world and, it's expensive – £500/$1000+.

Here is Sutherland figurine Pamela in underglaze pale blue and pink. BS: Thirties printed in black, height: 7". Sent in by Maureen from Cambridge. PG: £250-£275/$500-$550.

This rare painted piece depicts a woman feeding her geese. It is 6" tall, small crown backstamp, shape number 8. It is probably one of a pair and the first I have seen. Other 'unknown' pieces are paintings of sheep by F. Hancock and paintings of wild ducks by Lamonby. PG: £200/$400.

Sandy Powell tankard. This very rare piece turned up at auction in February 1996 and came on the open market with an asking price of £500/$1000. The small football in the handle commemorates his association with Accrington Stanley football club. The tune, a seaside song, was the comedian's signature tune. Sandy Powell jugs were made around 1939 but I have never seen one. The only reference I have of a Sandy Powell tankard is a magazine cutting which reports that one was sold at a Chester auction in October 1989 for £175/$350. That's about the time that Gracie Fields jugs were fetching a little over £100/$190!

Ivrine 1914-18 war officer. This Ivrine figure of an officer ready to lead his men 'over the top' was produced shortly after the end of the war and was embossed on the base 'Fieldings 9'. The owner bought it at the Three Counties showground fair in 1995 for £120/$240. Its value today: around £300/$600.

Gold Award Winner

Simon Fielding and Company won many awards at British Industries Fairs between the two world wars and they also picked up trophies at events throughout the world.

The Crown Devon success at the Panama Exhibition of 1915 is commemorated on cigarette card No 16 in a series of 50 called 'Modern British Pottery' which was issued by Ogden's, a branch of the Imperial Tobacco Company in the Thirties.

It was a Highland cattle-painted urn and cover some 23 inches high which took the gold medal and it is described on the back of the card 'as a translation into earthenware of the rich ornamentation of one of the best periods of fine china. The vellum-tinted body which forms the base of a large number of pieces makes a delightful medium for decoration. It has a very pleasing effect and well deserves its great popularity'.

Crown Devon had a second card – No. 18 – in the series, the only manufacturer to gain two entries. No. 18 is 'Devon Sylvan Lustrine ware' and the caption says 'This ware has a wonderfully lustrous ruby ground with butterflies painted by hand in brilliant colour and gold'.

The caption ends 'The Sylvan Lustrine ware is most suitable for the decoration of the modern home'. It was true then and it is still true today. Lustrine ware appears regularly at antique fairs and prices have not escalated as much as some products in the Crown Devon range. The Twenties saw the heyday of lustrine and two of the most popular patterns then – and now – are Sylvan butterflies on both powder blue and ruby grounds and Royal George by D. Cole showing a galleon on both powder blue and deep blue grounds. A fine example of a Royal George vase appeared at the 1996 new year Three Counties show at Malvern. It was on offer for between £70/$140 and £80/$160.

Crown Devon lustrine was decorated in more than 100 patterns and two firm favourites were the Mavis bird on a black ground and the Kingfisher bird on a ruby ground. I saw a Kingfisher vase, seven inches high and with a small gold backstamp and pearline interior at an antique fair in Cheshire in 1995. It was bought for £35/$70, about half its value. Prices vary considerably although the rarer patterns with the less common grounds of orange and green tend to fetch higher prices. There are always exceptions, of course, as a couple of years ago I paid £25/$50 for a ten-inch vase, pattern No. L63 – birds and mountains printed in black, shaded in black, orange lustre ground, black edge. At that price, lustrine has got to be a good investment.

Footnote. A diploma and silver medal were awarded to S. Fielding and Co., for their display of lustrine ware at a New Zealand exhibition at Dunedin in 1926.

Cigarette card No. 16 in a series of 50 of modern British pottery by Ogden's in the Thirties.

The 23-inch Crown Devon urn in Etna pattern similar to the one which won a gold medal in Panama in 1915. The face in the mirror? That of Graham Taylor who had just restored the vase to perfection.

Devon Pottery Patterns

Here is an alphabetical list of known patterns by Simon Fielding and Co., Devon Pottery, Stoke-on-Trent:

Pattern	Reg. No.	Pattern No.
Adams		0781
Aden		X744 & 0232
Albion	524189	0373
Alton		
Arden		
Ascot		
Athens		
Autumn		
Avon		
Ayr		
Azalea		
Balmoral		A245
Banff	577373	0598 & X31
Bath		
Bay		
Beta		
Birch		
Blenheim		
Blossom		
Bon(n)		03
Bray		
Briar		0532
Cam		X39
Carlton		
Carnation		863 & X163
Cedric		
Cecil		
Celtic		
Chelsea Crown		857 & 0762
Chelsea Royal		
Chelsea Black		0762
Chester		X564 & X646
Chintz		X35
Chrysanthemum (Royal Windsor)		229
Clifton		C50
Clyde		X380 & X248
Clio		
Cowes		X32
Commemoratives	563731	0584, 0578 & X189
Creeper		
Cretian		
Crown Devon	554725 & 414507	Various

Pattern	Reg. No.	Pattern No.
Cranesbill	785495	2442
Daisy		
Dee	658751	1035
Delhi		
Derby	287848	453
Dresden		
Derwent		
Don	662047	1076
Dolphin		
Doric		
Dora	629323	0871
Dove (black)		
Deva	541962	0376 Green stamp
Durbarry		
Durham		
Elm		Pattern nos. include A54, X67, X69, X89, X112, X113 & C215.
Elsa		
Ely		1721
Ena	629324	0971
Erin	611251	
Esk	607585	0731 & 0726
Etna	578617	0623
Eton	594089	0675
Eva	631528	0941
Exotic birds		0325
Fern		
Festoon		919
Fife		04
Filey		
Flora		
Florentine		
Frome		
Game		0671
Garland		
Gem	524189	0909
Glenn	516771	0150
Greba		
Grecian (solid blue)		
Greenland		
Haddon		X133

Pattern	Reg. No.	Pattern No.	Pattern	Reg. No.	Pattern No.
Heather			Rhodes		
Indian	376443	625 & 628	Rhyl		
	(Jan 26 1882)		Ribbon		
Iona			Riga		X877
Ivrine (figures)			Rio		
Jap		X822	Ripon		
Jersey	186839	C5, C44 &	Roses		831
	(1893)	C47	Rugby		
Kent	15--63	843	Ryde		745
	(1890)		Rye	RN202758	290
Kew Royal		A33	Salop		1119
Lady Hamilton			Saxon		X722 & X728
Lantern			Savoy		
Leeds			Sèvres	204438	240, 241 &
Leo				& 209757	242
Lynn		983	Shield (black)		
Lune	600413	0710	Silverine		
Lyons			Sligo		0693
Lustrine. Numerous patterns inc. Rustic,			Soleilian		
Aquatic, Fairy Castle, Fantasia Sylvan and			Spring	653216	1000
Royal George			Stella		
Magpie			Stockholm		
Mandarin			Suez		135
Marigold			Sydney		
Marshmallow			Tay		
Mavis (black)		1603	Tees		
May (19th century)		C1	Teck	644307	0965 & 6025
May (vellum)	689672	1186	Tenby		
Metz		124	Thames (19th century)		167
Nankin		X883	Thames (vellum)	658051	1025/6
Nasturtium			Togo		X752
Nevis			Tulip		
Nile			Turin		C57
Oban		C113	Usk		X1 & X66
Old Bow		W612	Victor		
Orchid	205288	327	Victorian		
	(1894)		Wells		X662
Orient		C227	Wem		X15
Oxon		X533, X511	Wick	648631	0992
Paisley			Wisteria		1371
Pearline			Wren		0431
Peel	708762	1202 & 2026	Wye (vellum)	635583	0560
Pegasus		1251	Wye (black)		0991
Peking					
Pendant	555509	0464			
Perth	622805	0876 & 0853			
Ramona					
Regatta					
Rex	686-	1260			

The Royals
Abbreviations:
LoC – Lion on crown backstamp
CoS – Crown on shield
LC – Large crown.

Name	Backstamp	Registration Number	Pattern Number
Clarence	LoC	205238 (1892)	996
Clarence	LoC	211861 (1893)	A23
Chelsea	CoS		
Devon	LC	Pink and blue	X482 and X543
Devon	LoC and LC	Orange and green	X712
Devon Blue	LC	Blue tint	X876
Essex	LoC	Blue border	998
		Green border	998
		Beige border	867
Eton	CoS		
Kent	CoS		
Kew	CoS		A33
Khaki	LoC		X184
Lorne	LoC		A24
Oxford	LoC		X94 and X164
Pearl	LC		0193
Persian	LoC		X76
Scotia	LoC		985
Stuart	LoC	White background	A28
		Vellum background	A29
Suffolk	LoC		
Sussex	LoC		A18
Tudor	LoC		X62
Windsor	CoS		851
York	CoS		

Footnote. Royal Stuart pieces have been seen with the following pattern numbers: Vase A27, smaller vase A29, pair of cake stands X376 and a teapot stand X368.

Known figures by Kathleen Parsons

157 – Maytime
165 – From Paris
166 – Gina
167 – Angela
168 – Rio Rita
172 – Caroline
173 – Grace
175 – Little Butterfly
176 – Sea Breeze
178 – Autumn Leaves

179 – Chaquita
180 – Christine
181 – June
185 – Sea Treasures
186 – Fairy Secrets
187 – Ninon
196 – Waltz Time
197 – Dancing Waves
198 – Summertime

Sutherland and other figures

60 – Beach Girl 12 inches
62 – Kiki 12 inches
121 – Windy Day 11 inches
124 – Bathing Girl 11 inches
125 – Yachting Twins 12 inches
127 – Rosemary 10 inches
128 – Betty 6 inches
129 – Lady Anne 7 inches
130 – Priscilla 6 inches
134 – Julie 7 inches
136 – Patricia 7 inches
137 – Gloria 9 inches
138 – Sheila 6 inches
139 – Marina 7 inches
140 – Juanita 7 inches
142 – Teresa 6 inches

143 – Greta 6 inches
144 – Wendy 6 inches
145 – Juliet 7 inches
146 – Sonia 4 inches
147 – Sleepy Boy
148 – Pauline 4 inches
149 – David 3 inches
150 – Tony 4 inches
154 – Spring 9 inches
155 – Yvonne 10 inches
156 – Carnival 9 inches
157 – Nina 4 inches
158 – Denise 7 and 4 inches
159 – Pamela 7 inches
160 – Natalie 8 inches
Marcelle 8 inches

References

Ceramic Art of Great Britain 1893 Jewitt
Pottery Gazette and Glass Trade Review
The Crown Devon Story 1991 Ray Barker
Crown Devon Susan Hill, Jazz Publications Ltd, Stratford upon Avon

Francis Joseph
'Collectors Register'

*At Francis Joseph we produce newsletters
containing details and updates of your
particular collectable. Registration is free
and you only have to write or call us
to be placed on our register.*

**If you have purchased this book direct from us –
there is no need to register –
we already have your details and will
keep you up to date.**

*Also, if you have any details which would be helpful
in the next edition of this book, then please write in
with them at the same time*

Telephone: 0181 318 9580

Francis Joseph
15 St Swithuns Road
London SE13 6RW
Telephone: 0181 318 9580
Fax: 0181 318 1987

The nude they dare not take home!!!

Here is Dawn, Number 171 in the series of Nude Figures produced by Fieldings. She is one of the daring figures illustrated in a 1930s brochure labelled "Crown Devon Figures and Lamps modelled by Kathleen Parsons". It is a must for all Crown Devon Collectors.

This brochure along with a 12-page booklet "Crown Devon figures, lamps and gift suggestions" and an illustrated leaflet "Champion Dogs Heads Studies" is available from the author, Ray Barker. The price is £5 including packing and postage and orders should be sent to 25 Kings End Road, Powick, Worcester WR2 4RB. Cheques should be made payable to A. R. Barker. Overseas orders, add £3.

Says Ray: "Kathleen Parsons told me that when the series was introduced, some of the reps were very reluctant to take their samples home as their wives might be quite upset.

X